TURNING POINTS in Welsh History 1485–1914

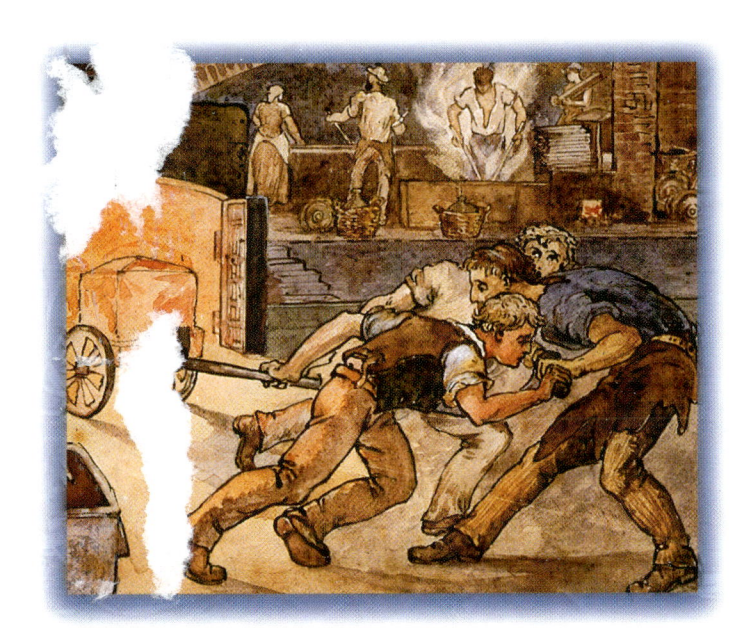

Stuart Broomfield and Euryn Madoc-Jones

University of Wales Press
Cardiff
2004

© ACCAC
(Qualifications, Curriculum & Assessment Authority for Wales), 2004

All rights reserved. No part of this book may be reproduced, stored in a retrieval system, or transmitted, in any form or by any means, electronic, mechanical, photocopying, recording or otherwise, without clearance from the University of Wales Press, 10 Columbus Walk, Brigantine Place, Cardiff, CF10 4UP.
www.wales.ac.uk/press

British Library
Cataloguing-in-Publication Data
A catalogue record for this book is available from the British Library.

ISBN
0–7083–1828–2 English-language version
0–7083–1843–6 Welsh-language version

The rights of Stuart Broomfield and Euryn Madoc-Jones to be identified as authors of this work have been asserted by them in accordance with sections 77 and 78 of the Copyright, Designs and Patents Act 1988.

Published with the financial assistance of ACCAC (Qualifications, Curriculum & Assessment Authority for Wales)

Design: Olwen Fowler
Original illustrations: Brett Breckon
Translation of Welsh version:
   Glenys Roberts, Araul
Picture research: Sue Charles
Production: Liz Powell, Nicky Roper
Project manager and editor: Ceinwen Jones

Printed in Malta by Gutenberg Press

Contents

	page
What are turning points?	4
Turning points in Welsh history	6
The History Skills Gang	7

Part 1: 1485–1760

1.1	What was life in Wales like between 1485 and 1760?	10
1.2	Should Henry VII be a Welsh hero?	28
1.3	Why was the translation of the Bible into Welsh in 1588 an important event in Welsh history?	43

Part 2: 1760–1914

2.1	How did Wales change between 1760 and 1914?	65
2.2	Why was Wales on the move?	86
2.3	Were the Welsh people troublemakers in the nineteenth century?	121
2.4	How was Wales changing at the start of the twentieth century?	142

Glossary	164
Notes for teachers	166
Index	170
Acknowledgements	174

What are turning points?

Turning points in history are very important events or developments that change the lives of people in a big way.

Can you remember when you moved from primary school to secondary school? This led to many changes in your life. The move was a turning point in your life.

TASK

In groups discuss how the move was a turning point in your life. You need to remember what your life was like before going to secondary school and what your life has been like since. Think about the following things: friends, teachers, social life, travel to school, and so on.

Sometimes peoples' lives are changed because of an important invention – the invention of the mobile phone is a good example.

If you have a mobile phone what do you use it for? Why is it important in your life? Try and remember a time before you had a mobile phone. How was your life different then?

Think!
Discuss with a partner other inventions that have made changes. How did they change people's lives?

Turning points in history

The development of television is a good example of a turning point in the past.

Think!
What did people do in the evenings before television was introduced in the early 1950s?
- How did peoples' front rooms change?
- How did their eating habits change?
- How did their leisure activities change?
- What happened to newspapers as a result of television?

TASK

In groups discuss the events/developments/inventions on the list below. How did they make big changes in peoples' lives? Remember! Think about life before the turning point and life afterwards.
- the invention of fire
- the Norman Conquest (revision!)
- the invention of the motor car
- travelling by air

In this book we shall be studying some significant events in the history of Wales.
In Year 7 you will have learned about the death in 1282 of Llywelyn ap Gruffydd, known as Y Llyw Olaf (the Last Prince). This event was a major turning point in Welsh history.

Llywelyn ap Gruffydd.

After 1282:
- King Edward I of England conquered Wales.
- All of Wales was now ruled by the English king or people appointed by him.
- Great castles were built in north and mid Wales where Llywelyn had been strong.
- New taxes had to be paid to the English king.
- Welsh people were to be tried according to English law and the Welsh language could not be used in the courts.

Turning points in history can change peoples' lives in different ways:
Economically – to do with money
Socially – to do with the way you live your life
Culturally – to do with your language, ideas and beliefs
Politically – to do with the way you are ruled or governed.

Think!
Look back at all the examples of turning points already mentioned. In pairs find an example of each type of turning point – economic, social, cultural and political.

A turning point can be one event or a series of events

Key word
appointed: given a job or title

Some turning points can make changes to peoples' lives suddenly or quickly. Others take years to have an effect.

When Prince Llywelyn was killed in 1282, people would very quickly have become aware of changes in their lives. If they lived in Harlech, a great castle would have been built on their doorstep. Local people would have been forced to work for the English to build the castle. Soldiers would have appeared in the village. People would have been stopped and searched.

Harlech Castle, built by King Edward I.

With the invention of the motor car, change was much more gradual. Few people had cars at the start of the twentieth century. It was not until the 1950s that ordinary people could afford them. In the 1960s great road-building programmes were started. The first motorways were built, the first Severn Bridge was opened, and bypasses were built around cities and towns. Eventually, everybody's life was affected, whether they had a motor car or not.

Think!
Look back at all the examples of turning points discussed above. With a partner think about an example of a turning point that introduced a sudden change and one which introduced changes over a long period of time.
   Can you think of other examples, either from your own experience or from other topics which you have studied in history?

Turning points in Welsh history

Turning points in history come in many different forms and affect people in many different ways. This book will examine events and developments in Wales in the years between 1485 and 1914. These are some of the puzzles we shall explore:

Did Henry VII care about Wales? Did it make any difference to Wales that someone with Welsh connections became King of England?

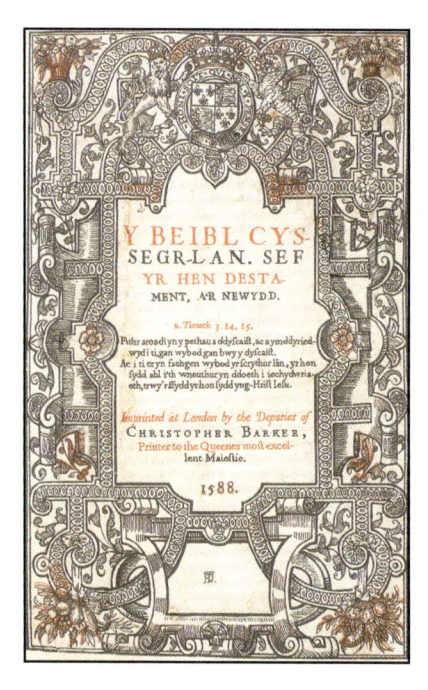

Why did the publication of the Bible in Welsh matter so much?

Why did so many people leave their homes and make new lives for themselves in the early nineteenth century?

Were Welsh people troublemakers in the nineteenth century or did they have good reasons to protest?

What did it mean to be Welsh at the start of the twentieth century?

The History Skills Gang

Time to meet the gang!

Throughout this book you will see some characters appearing and reappearing. They are there to help you, to show you what skills you might need for that part of the book.

Captain Chronology

puts things like days, years, centuries, periods in order so that they make sense, and also creates time lines:

| 1485 | 1500 | 1588 | 1600 | 1700 | 1760 | 1800 | 1839 | 1900 | 1913 | 2000 |

Henry VII becomes King (1485)

Bible published in Welsh (1588)

Early inventions in Industrial Revolution (around 1760)

Chartist protest at Newport (1839)

Exports of coal from Cardiff at their highest ever (1913)

Note that centuries can be tricky!
This table shows the names of centuries:

Century	C	Years
Fifteenth	15th	1400–1499
Sixteenth	16th	1500–1599
Seventeenth	17th	1600–1699
Eighteenth	18th	1700–1799
Nineteenth	19th	1800–1899
Twentieth	20th	1900–1999

Chronology is very important to history. We must get things in order if we are to understand how and why things happened, and what life was like in different historical periods.

Professor Info uses

information to show that he understands things:
- why something happened
- what were the results
- why some things have changed
- why some things have stayed the same
- why some things are important.

Professor Info will point out where to find the answers to these questions. **Remember**, knowing a lot of facts does not necessarily make you a good historian. A good historian uses these facts to explain things.

Key word
contemporary: from the time of the events

Why did Henry VII become king in 1485?

Inspector Evidence looks

at evidence to find out what we think happened.

We can look at different types of evidence, such as pictures, written documents, objects and buildings.

These might be contemporary evidence from the time of the events, or evidence given by historians from later times.

With written evidence, for example, we must ask:
What is the evidence? (**C**ontent)
When was it written? (**O**rigin)
Who wrote it and why? (**P**urpose)

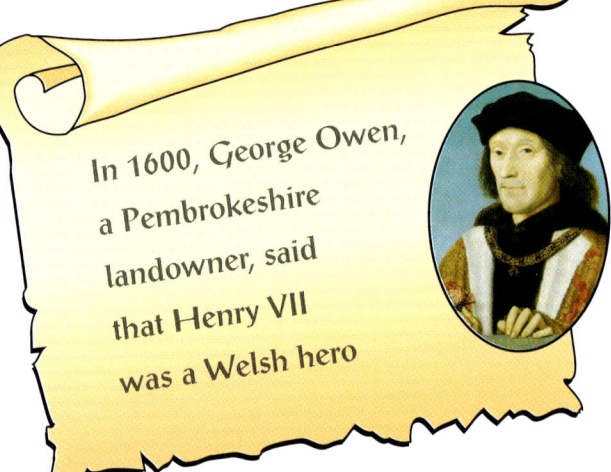

In 1600, George Owen, a Pembrokeshire landowner, said that Henry VII was a Welsh hero

So Inspector Evidence helps us to look at **C**ontent, **O**rigin and **P**urpose of different pieces of evidence. Remember that Inspector Evidence is a **COP**!

Ivan Interpretation makes history fun because he helps you to develop your own account of history based on the evidence you have seen.

For example, some people think that King Henry VII was a Welsh hero. Other people think he was a traitor to Wales.

Ivan Interpretation helps us to understand why people have different points of view about someone like Henry VII.

Confused? Then you must look at the evidence and decide on your own interpretation.

Key words
traitor: a person who betrays his/her own side
point of view: idea, opinion

Ms Organized is a very important member of the gang. She helps us to select information and organize it in an orderly way, so that we can make sense of events and people's lives in the past.

She can organize things in many ways:

PARAGRAPHS
sentences
ESSAYS
graphs
CHARTS
ICT PRESENTATIONS
posters
maps

PART 1 1485–1760

1.1 What was life in Wales like between 1485 and 1760?

Key word

landscape: what the land looks like

On pages 12–21 there are four sets of picture sources. Each set of picture sources is followed by a set of written sources. They have been grouped together under four headings:
- People
- Homes
- Ideas and beliefs
- Landscape

Looking at picture sources

All the sources are **contemporary evidence**. This means that they come from the period of history being talked about, in this case 1485 to 1760. For example, the portrait of the Mansel family (see page 12) was painted in 1625, and the memorial to Margaret Mercer (see page 18) was built in 1610. The photograph of Gwydir Castle (see page 15) shows a section of the building that was built around 1500.

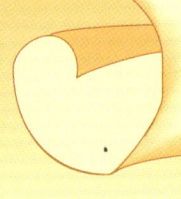

TASK 1

In groups look closely at **ONE** set of picture sources – People **or** Homes **or** Ideas and beliefs **or** Landscape.

1. Write down what you can **definitely** see in the sources. For example in the picture of Katheryn of Berain (no. 2 on page 13) you will see that her left hand is on top of a skull. Describe her clothing and other items in the portrait.

2. When you have written down this information, discuss with your group what the evidence tells you about your theme. For example, if your topic is 'Ideas and beliefs', one thing you may decide is that churches were important buildings in towns.

3. Copy out the table in the map on the right (or use the outline provided in the activity pack), and under the heading of your theme make four or five bullet points about your topic. An example has been given under the heading of landscape.

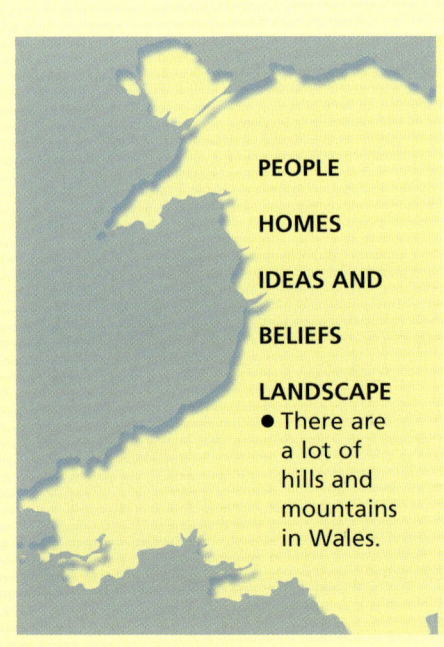

PEOPLE

HOMES

IDEAS AND BELIEFS

LANDSCAPE
- There are a lot of hills and mountains in Wales.

Wales, 1485–1760, based on a selection of contemporary evidence

TASK 1 (continued)

4 One person needs to report back to the rest of the class with the information that the group have collected. Remember! Only use the information that you can definitely find in the sources.

5 When each group reports back, listen carefully to what is being said. On your copy of the table note down the main points made by the speakers.

peaceful, violent, rich, flat, happy, poor, dirty, overcrowded, religious, sad, wet, mountainous, beautiful

TASK 2

You now have a general idea about Wales in the period 1485–1760. Above are some words that you could use to describe Wales in these years.

1 In pairs choose the best five words to describe the Wales that you see in the pictures.

2 Write down three new words that you could add to the list. You could use a dictionary to help you.

3 Make a class list of ten words to describe the Wales you can see in the pictures.

The pictures show Wales as a land with beautiful scenery full of wealthy people who lived in big houses. But is this true?
- Only wealthy people had their portraits painted.
- Only wealthy people had large stone houses built which have survived to the present day.
- Only wealthy people had large tombs built.
- Artists painted to earn a living; therefore they only painted for the rich.

We can now look at a selection of written contemporary sources (sources written at the time) on pages 14, 17, 19 and 21. It will be interesting to see if these give a different picture of Wales in this period.

TASK 3

1 Before looking at the written sources, copy out another table like the one on page 10.

2 Read through each set of **written sources** (People, Homes, Ideas and beliefs, and Landscape) one set at a time. Pick out any new and interesting things that you did not see in the picture sources and write them down, using bullet heads, on the table that you have made.

People

Looking at picture sources

1. Sir Thomas Mansel of Margam, his wife and their daughter (about 1625).

Sir Rice Mansel of Oxwich Castle, the Purchaser of Margam. Anne his Wife, Dau. of Sir Giles Bridges with Catharine their Dau.

2. Katheryn of Berain, 1568.

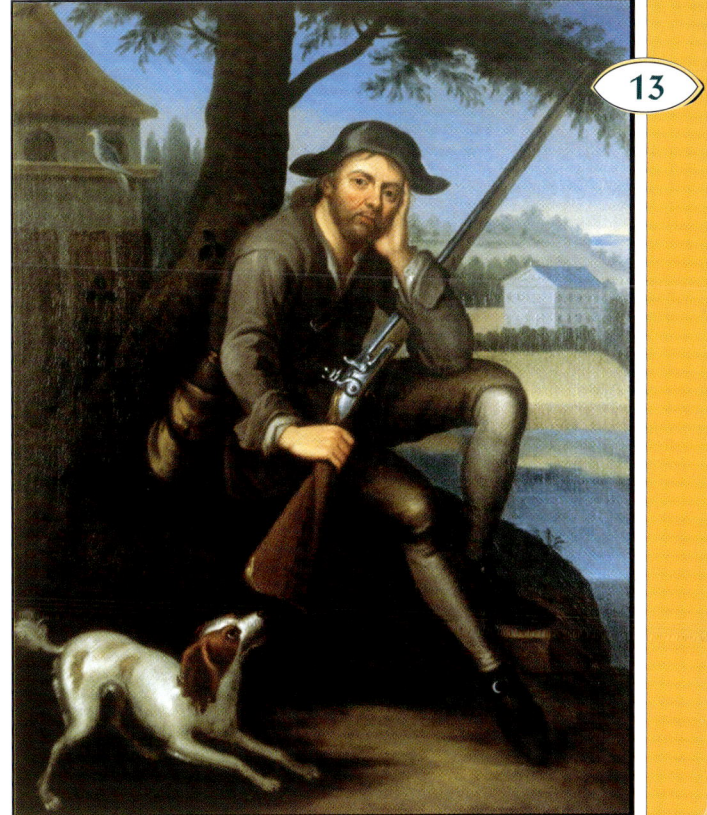

3. Edward Herbert, First Baron Herbert of Chirbury (about 1610).

4. The gamekeeper at Edwinsford, Carmarthenshire (1725).

People

Looking at written sources

> **Key words**
>
> **Justice of the Peace:** a member of the gentry appointed to be responsible for law and order
> **vagabond:** a homeless person, a tramp
> **gentry:** the landowning class
> **gentleman:** a member of the gentry

Source 1.
From a letter written by a Justice of the Peace in Anglesey (sixteenth century):

We have a large number of beggars and vagabonds who do no work, wandering over all the country from house to house, and from place to place.

Source 2.
George Owen, from his book *The Description of Pembrokeshire*, 1603 (George Owen was a gentleman, a member of the gentry):

The common sort of people, the greatest number, I find to be very poor and simple, short of growth, broad and shrubby. They are forced to endure the heat of the sun which burns their faces, hands, legs and feet. And then with the cold, frost, snow, hail and wind they are so tormented having the skin of their legs, hands, face and feet all in chinks and chaps [cracks and splits].

Source 3.
William Williams of Beaumaris, 1674, writing about Sir Richard Bulkeley, an Elizabethan gentleman:

He kept many servants and attendants. Two lackeys in livery [servants in uniform] always ran by his horse; he never went from home without 20 or 24 to attend him.

Source 4.
George Owen was an important landowner in Pembrokeshire. He owned a number of farms. This is his list of the people he employed at the farm of Cwrt Eglwyswrw:

People in household and daily charge of the farm.
The ploughman or chief servant
His wife
One other man servant
Two ploughboys
One shepherd
Two labouring maids

Homes

Looking at picture sources

5. Gwydir Castle (built about 1500).

6. The Long Gallery at Powys Castle, Montgomeryshire (about 1590).

7. Llannerch, Denbighshire (painted about 1662).

8. Plas Mawr, Conwy, built in the sixteenth century in Conwy town.

Homes

Looking at written sources

Source 5.
Description of an Anglesey estate from the 1630s:

The houses are but sheds, not fit for a man to rest himself in for an hour or two much less to lodge in.

Source 6.
Household goods of a small farmhouse near Haverfordwest (1592):

1 cauldron; 3 pans; frying pan; 5 dishes; 1 pot; 2 candlesticks; 1 cupboard; 1 spinning wheel; 1 pack of cards; 1 table; 1 form; 1 brush; 1 branding iron; 2 bedsteads; 2 pairs of blankets; 1 coverlet; 1 bolster; 2 brass vessels; 1 bucket; 1 hutch.

Source 7.
Extract from Leland's *Itinerary in Wales*, written between 1536 and 1539:

George Mathew a man of pretty lands dwelling at Radyr has a park with deer newly made above Radyr.

Source 8.
Description of Bachegraig in Caernarfonshire, built in 1567:

It consists of a mansion, and three sides, inclosing a square court. The first floor consists of a vast hall and parlour: the rest of it rises into six wonderful stories, including the cupola [dome above the roof of a building] and forms from the second floor the figure of a pyramid.

Ideas and beliefs

Looking at picture sources

9. The Church of St Andrew, Presteigne (painted about 1680).

11. Memorial to Margaret Mercer, St Mary's Church, Tenby (1610).

10. The title page of the Bible in Welsh.

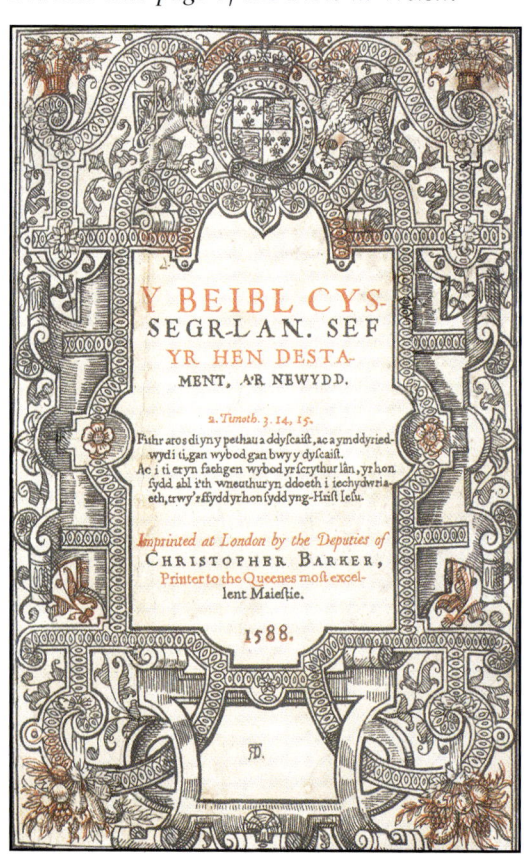

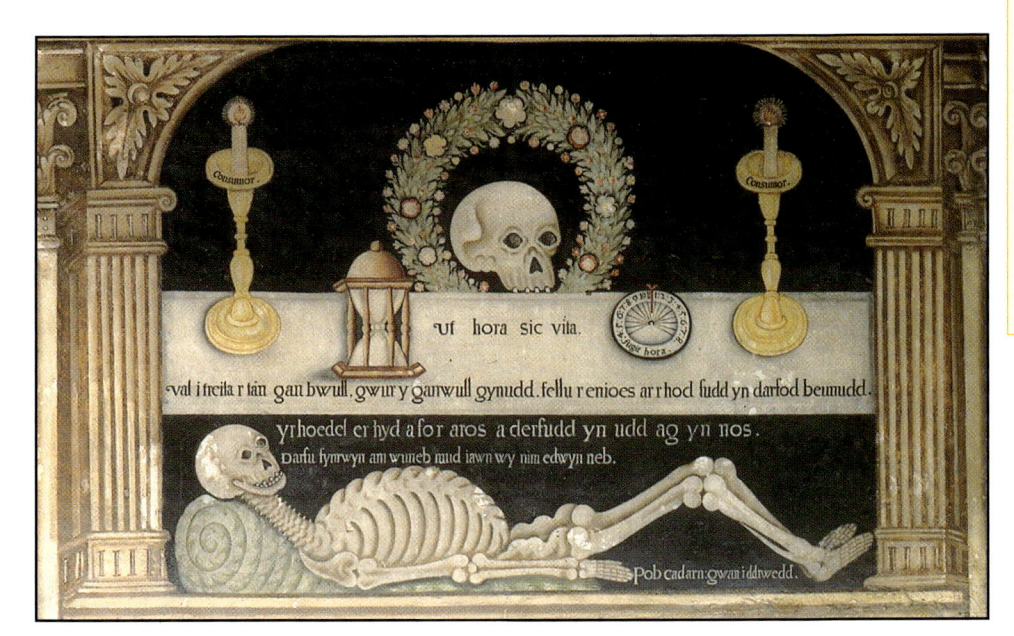

Key words

Catholic: a member of the Church of Rome under the leadership of the Pope.
Protestants: those who broke away from the Catholic Church in the sixteenth century.
execution: to put someone to death as a punishment

12. A memorial at Rug Chapel (about 1637).

Ideas and beliefs

Looking at written sources

Source 9.
Record of a punishment for stealing cheese in Ffestiniog in 1557:

Margaret Madog stole a cheese from Lewis Williams. Her punishment is to be flogged and then nailed by her ear in the market place at Caernarfon.

Source 10.
From Humphrey Llwyd's *Breviary of Britain* (1573):

The water at St Winifred's Well [at Holywell] is very pleasant. Many who wash in the water were cured of many illnesses that they were born with.

Source 11.
From the *Book of Martyrs* (1563), by John Foxe, a Protestant writer:

In these miserable days of Queen Mary, William Nichol, an honest good simple man, was arrested by the champions of the pope and on the 9th day of April, 1558, was burnt at Haverfordwest in Wales.

Source 12.
An account of the death of Richard Gwyn, a Catholic, on 15 October 1584:

Then the judge passed sentence on him, that on the following Thursday (when there was usually a crowd of people present because of the market) Gwyn should be dragged to the place of execution, hanged until half dead, beheaded, disembowelled and his body quartered.

Landscape

Looking at picture sources

13. Dinefwr Castle, Llandeilo (about 1670).

14. Chepstow, Monmouthshire (painted 1680–90).

15. Rhaidder Fawr, a waterfall near Penmaen-mawr, Gwynedd (1750).

Landscape

Looking at written sources

Source 13.
From a diary by Celia Fiennes describing a visit to Flintshire in 1688:

The place is called Flintshire. It is a hilly place with many very high hills where the people speak Welsh. They go barefoot and bare-legged.

Source 14.
An extract from Edward Lhuyd's *Geographical Dictionary of Wales* (1696):

Between Tregaron and Builth it is for the most part mountainous, rocky, barren; but breeds plenty of good sheep.

Source 15.
From the letters of Bernardino de Mendoza of Spain, who visited Wales in 1586:

In south and north Wales the land is rather mountainous but the country is rich in sheep and cattle. There is plenty of wheat and the ports are numerous and good.

Source 16.
George Owen, *The Dialogue of the Government of Wales* (1594):

The people are grown to be of great wealth. Now we see the old castles of Wales all in ruin and decay, and on the contrary the houses of the gentlemen to flourish.

TASK 4

Copy out the table below. You have used it twice before. You have to write about each of the themes again. This time your task is harder. Write about each of the themes using the information from the two tables that you have already completed.

- PEOPLE
- HOMES
- IDEAS AND BELIEFS
- LANDSCAPE

When you write information down using more than one source the process is called **synthesis**. People who write history often do this with a large number of different sources.

Think!
- Why do you think that historians try and use as many different sources as possible?
- Why, in some cases do historians have to use only one or two sources?

The first description that you made of Wales in the years 1485–1760 from the picture sources has probably changed because of the new information that you have read in the written accounts. This does not mean that you have an accurate picture. Putting together information about Wales 1485–1760 is like creating a massive jigsaw. You still only have a few of the pieces.

Remember that when studying this period you have fewer pictures and documents than for the twentieth century. These pictures and documents tell us mostly about the lives of rich people.

Because there is more evidence about the rich, it is therefore possible to learn more about a gentleman like Edward Herbert of Chirbury than about the men and women who lived on his estate.

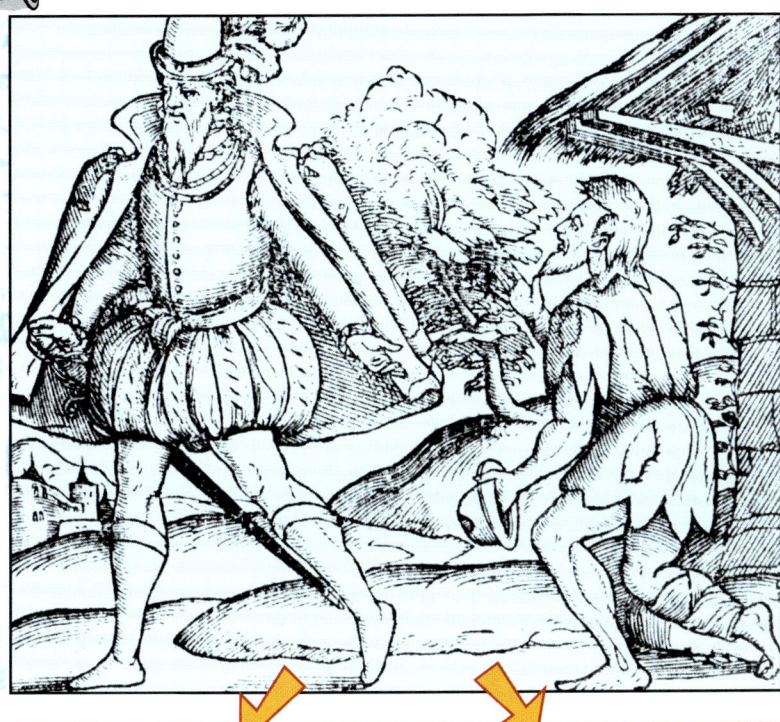

A gentleman

Historians know quite a lot about me

portraits
painting of my house
my house is still standing in the 21st century
some of my furniture has been kept
my diary
my household accounts
my letters
my will

A poor person

Historians know hardly anything about me

no portrait (I cannot pay an artist)
no painting of my house
my house has disappeared by the 21st century
no furniture has survived (I had very little anyway)
no diary (I cannot read and write)
no household accounts (I have no money)
no letters
no will (because I have nothing to leave to my children)

With the lives of the poor, you have to think carefully about the evidence that we have. Much of the evidence about poor people comes from records of law courts.

Look at Source 9 (p. 19). This is from a court record. There are a lot of these records. What impression do you think that they give about poor people at this time? Is this a fair impression or not?

Historians often have to work out what life was like in the past or what individual people were like. Sometimes it is impossible to find an answer to some questions if the evidence is not there. Historians suggest what might have happened based on the information that is available.

For example, have a look at the picture of the Mansel family of Margam (picture 1 on page 12). The picture tells you what clothes Thomas Mansel and his family wore, but what kind of people were they? Can you make some suggestions?

TASK 5

1. Look at the picture of Chepstow in 1680–90 (no. 14 on page 20). What does this picture tell you about travel and transport in Wales at this time?

2. Think about the following questions. Your only evidence is in the sources. You will find some evidence to answer the first question but you will have to make your own suggestions to answer question b.
   a. How would people have travelled from Chepstow in south-east Wales to visit the Wynn family who lived at Gwydir Castle in north-west Wales?
   b. Would the journey have been difficult? If so, why? (Looking at the Landscape section on pages 20–1 may help you.)

Work, 1485–1760

The picture sources and written sources have been sorted under four headings: People, Homes, Ideas and beliefs and Landscape. It would be possible, however, to group them according to the theme of **Work**.

TASK 6

1. Look again at the following four pictures:
   Edward Herbert of Chirbury (no. 3)
   The gamekeeper at Edwinsford (no. 4)
   Llannerch, Denbighshire (no. 7)
   Chepstow 1680–90 (no. 14).
   Note down what you can see and what you can suggest about work in this period from these picture sources.

2. Now look again at the following written sources: Source 1, Source 2, Source 3, Source 4 and Source 6.
   Note down what the sources tell you about work and what you can suggest.

3. Now you are in a position to write a few sentences about work in this period. You can synthesize the information from the visual sources and from the written sources.

Looking at what historians have written about this period

The exercises that follow will try to give you more help in understanding this period by looking at accounts written by modern historians about the people, homes, ideas and beliefs, landscape and work in this period.

Key words

uplands: mountainous, high land
grazing: feeding cattle and other farm animals on grass growing in the field

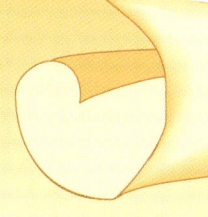

TASK 7

Read the description below by Peter Gaunt, a modern historian. He has read a number of sources and looked at pictures before writing this account. He describes the geography of Wales in 1640:

Geography divides Wales into two parts. Almost two-thirds comprises fairly barren uplands where the generally wet, cool climate and often poor soils meant that in the seventeenth century this land was suitable for little more than fairly rough grazing. The uplands were thinly populated, dotted with lonely farms and occasional small villages, and crossed by few roads.

The population was approaching 400,000 in 1640. Only about 10 per cent lived in towns. No town was large, and in our eyes most would be thought of as only villages. Wrexham, with perhaps 2,500 people, was the largest town in north Wales, Carmarthen the largest in the south.

1. Look at the pictures and the written sources on 'Landscape' (pages 20–1). Make a list of the evidence in these sources that Peter Gaunt may have used.

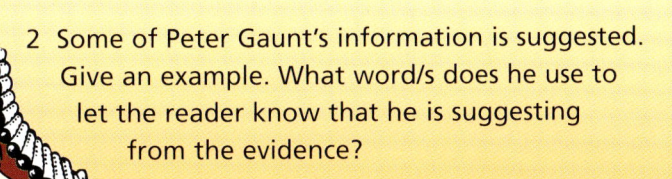

2. Some of Peter Gaunt's information is suggested. Give an example. What word/s does he use to let the reader know that he is suggesting from the evidence?

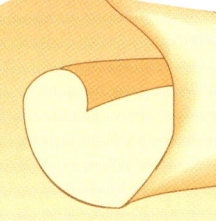

TASK 8

Matthew Griffiths, writing in 'Land, Life and Belief, 1415–1642' in 2000, describes the differences between the rich and the poor:

In the Tudor and Stuart countryside of Wales a greater gap opened up between the relatively well off and the poor.

The rise of the gentry, and their wealth, was portrayed to the world by their houses. The better off were able to improve their comfort. At the bottom end of the social scale the position of the 50 per cent or more of families who ranked as the poorest farmers, cottagers and labourers was bleak. Certainly none of their houses survive – and many homes can have been little more than temporary shelters.

1. What picture and written evidence supports Matthew Griffiths's description of the rich?

2. What evidence supports his description of the poor?

3. What difference, if any, do you notice about the evidence about the rich and the evidence about the poor?

4. What new information does Matthew Griffiths give that is not in the sources?

5. Does Matthew Griffiths make any suggestions? If so, why does he have to do this?

TASK 9

Professor Gareth Elwyn Jones, author of the textbook *Tudor Wales* (1986), wrote this about religion in the Tudor period:

During the Tudor Period, the Church, Roman Catholic or Protestant, played an important part in people's lives. For some, on both sides, it was so important that they were prepared to die in agony for their beliefs. For far more people the Church was a matter of habit.

1. Read written Sources 11 and 12 again about William Nichol and Richard Gwyn. How do they support the statement made by Gareth Elwyn Jones?

2. What was the same about William Nichol and Richard Gwyn and what was different?

3. What do you think Gareth Elwyn Jones means when he writes that many people went to church as 'a matter of habit'?

4. Gareth Elwyn Jones says that some people were prepared to die for their beliefs. He also suggests that most people went to church as 'a matter of habit'. Why does he have to **suggest** this?

After studying this chapter you should have a general idea about life in Wales during the period 1485–1760.

- Wales was a mainly rural country with a small population.

- Some very rich people, the gentry, lived in large houses and owned a lot of land. The majority of people were poor.

- Most people worked on the land, either for a rich master, or to grow enough food to feed themselves and their families.

- Most people were Christians and went to church, but people had different ideas about how they should worship God.

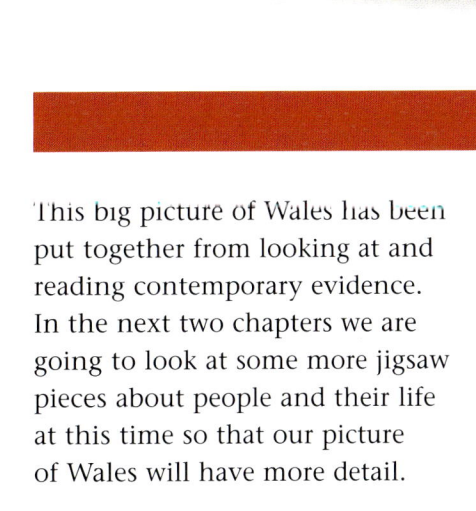

This big picture of Wales has been put together from looking at and reading contemporary evidence. In the next two chapters we are going to look at some more jigsaw pieces about people and their life at this time so that our picture of Wales will have more detail.

1.2 Should Henry VII be a Welsh hero?

Key word

invade: attack and enter (from somewhere outside)
reign: time during which a king or queen rules a country

This is a photograph of a sculpture of Henry VII. It is in City Hall, Cardiff. It is in a collection of sculptures remembering great people from Welsh history.

Professor Info:

King Henry VII was born in Pembroke Castle. His grandfather was a Welshman, and his family name was Tudor. In 1485 he invaded from France and landed his army on the coast of Pembrokeshire in south-west Wales. He marched through Wales on his way to England to meet the English king in battle. He defeated and killed King Richard III at the Battle of Bosworth Field. After the battle he became King of England and lived until 1509. He brought much needed peace to England and Wales. His story appears in many books about Welsh history.

One hundred years after Henry VII became king, George Owen, a wealthy Pembrokeshire landowner, praised him. He said that Henry was a great leader who had helped the people of Wales.

Not everyone agrees with this view of Henry VII. Alun Roberts, a writer, published a book called *Welsh National Heroes* in 2002. Henry VII is not included.

In this investigation into his life we are going to examine whether Henry deserves to be in a collection of Welsh heroes. At the same time we shall also consider whether his reign should be regarded as a turning point in the history of Wales. What changed in Wales after he came to the throne?

Henry VII, painted in 1505

Wales before Henry Tudor

Key words

bard: a poet who usually sang verses and played the harp

prophecy: foretelling of the future

Owain Glyndŵr

The picture shows a sculpture of Owain Glyndŵr. This sculpture also stands in the collection of Welsh heroes in Cardiff City Hall. Owain led a great revolt against the King of England between 1400 and 1408. During the revolt King Henry IV passed special laws against the Welsh:

- No Welsh person could carry weapons.
- No Welsh person could live in a town.
- No Welsh person could hold important jobs.
- The laws applied to English people married to Welsh people.

Some historians think that these laws were hardly used, but they were still in the lawbooks throughout the fifteenth century. Welsh bards wrote poems in which they called for a 'saviour' to come to free the Welsh people and improve their lives – the 'son of prophecy' ('Mab Darogan').

The Wars of the Roses, 1455–1485

These were years of civil war in England and Wales. Two families fought for the throne. These were the Lancastrians and the Yorkists. The Tudor family were on the side of the Lancastrians. Welsh soldiers fought on both sides during the wars because both the Lancastrian and the Yorkist families owned castles and large estates of land in different parts of Wales.

The emblems of the Yorkist (white rose) and Lancastrian (red rose) families.

Wales during the fifteenth century was wild and dangerous. It was difficult to travel, robbery was common and most people were very poor. Welsh towns were small and not very wealthy.

Who was Henry Tudor?

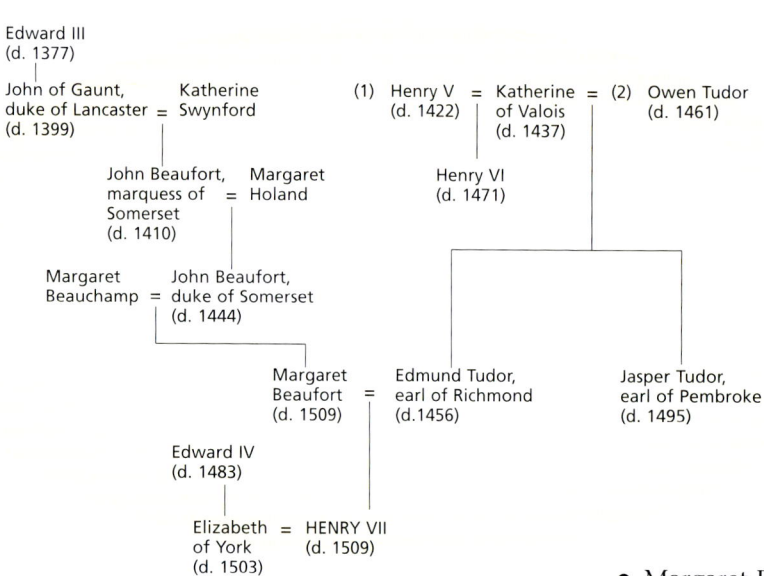

Key words

ancestors: forefathers, people from whom you are descended

heiress: a woman who inherits a lot of money or land

guardian: someone who looks after a child in place of parents

Here is Henry's family tree:

```
Edward III
(d. 1377)
   |
John of Gaunt,           Katherine        (1) Henry V  =  Katherine  = (2)  Owen Tudor
duke of Lancaster  =  Swynford                (d. 1422)    of Valois         (d. 1461)
(d. 1399)                                                  (d. 1437)
            |                                      |
      John Beaufort,    Margaret              Henry VI
      marquess of   =  Holand                 (d. 1471)
      Somerset
      (d. 1410)
            |
      Margaret       John Beaufort,
      Beauchamp  =   duke of Somerset
                     (d. 1444)
                  |
              Margaret         Edmund Tudor,         Jasper Tudor,
              Beaufort     =   earl of Richmond      earl of Pembroke
              (d. 1509)        (d.1456)              (d. 1495)
                  |
              Edward IV
              (d. 1483)
                  |
              Elizabeth    =    HENRY VII
              of York           (d. 1509)
              (d. 1503)
```

Remember, between 1455 and 1485 there was a civil war in England and Wales. The Yorkists fought against the Lancastrians.

- Owen Tudor was the grandfather of Henry Tudor. He came from Penmynydd in Anglesey and claimed that his ancestors were Welsh princes. Although he was only a royal servant, he married Katherine of Valois, the widow of King Henry V. His sons therefore had the same mother as the Lancastrian King Henry VI. Owen fought on the Lancastrian side in the Wars of the Roses and was beheaded by the Yorkists in 1461.

- Edmund Tudor was the father of Henry Tudor. He married a rich, thirteen-year-old heiress, Margaret Beaufort. He was imprisoned by the Yorkists in Carmarthen Castle in 1456 and died of disease shortly after being released. Henry was born a few months later.

The brass picture of Edmund on his grave in Carmarthen.

- Margaret Beaufort was Henry Tudor's mother. She gave birth to Henry shortly before her fourteenth birthday. Soon afterwards she remarried and did not see Henry again until 1471 when he was fourteen. Henry Tudor's only real claim to the throne came through her and she worked hard to support him.

- Jasper Tudor was the uncle of Henry Tudor and became his guardian. Jasper was the strongest Lancastrian leader in Wales during the Wars of the Roses.

Margaret Beaufort, Henry's mother.

Think!

Family trees are very complicated. Try and answer the following questions.

1. Some say that Henry Tudor was only one-quarter Welsh. Have a close look at his family tree. Explain what this means.

2. Henry Tudor's claim to the throne of England and Wales was because of his mother's relatives, not his father's. Try and explain this statement.

3. How were Henry VI and Henry VII related?

Henry Tudor's early life story, 1457–1485

Key words
live in exile: forced to live outside his own country
assassination: murder of an important person (often for political reasons)

Birth
Henry Tudor was born in Pembroke Castle in January 1457. Henry's uncle, Jasper, took care of him.

Pembroke Castle

Prison!
When the Yorkist King Edward IV became king in 1461, 4-year-old Henry was captured by Yorkists at Pembroke and taken to Raglan Castle where he was kept as a prisoner until 1470. His uncle Jasper escaped to France.

Raglan Castle

A Lancastrian king in control again!
In 1469 the Lancastrians fought back and defeated the Yorkists. The Lancastrian Henry VI, Henry Tudor's uncle, became king again. Jasper Tudor returned from France and Henry left Raglan Castle to join him.

A Yorkist king again!
In 1471 the Yorkists captured King Henry VI and killed his son. Henry VI died in the Tower of London and the Yorkist, King Edward IV, became king for a second time.

Henry VI

Henry escapes to Brittany
Henry Tudor, aged sixteen, became the next Lancastrian male with the best claim to be king. He was now in danger from the Yorkists. He and his uncle Jasper escaped from Pembroke Castle to Tenby. From there they sailed to Brittany. Henry lived in exile in Brittany and France from 1471 until 1485. He escaped several assassination attempts by Yorkist spies.

Richard III takes control
In 1483 King Edward IV died. Shortly afterwards his children, King Edward V and Richard of York (the 'Princes in the Tower'), disappeared. It is thought that they were murdered in the Tower of London, but we cannot be sure who killed them. Their uncle was crowned King Richard III.

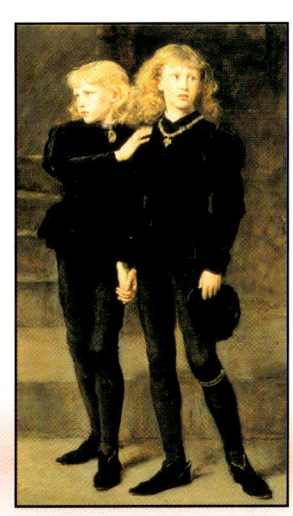

Invasion from France
In 1485 Henry decided to attack King Richard III to claim the crown of England for himself. He received money from the French king to pay an army of about 5,000 soldiers who sailed with him from France to Wales.

The Princes in the Tower

Key word

revenge: hurt done to someone in return for a wrong or injury already suffered

TASK

This exercise will help you to understand all the information about Henry Tudor's early life and to understand the order in which events took place (chronology).

Put these events into the correct chronological order and fill in the information missing from the table:

Date	King and family	Important event	Where Henry Tudor was	How Henry was affected
1485	_____	Henry gets support from the French king	France	Henry prepares to invade Wales and England
1457	Henry VI (Lancaster)	Henry Tudor is born	_____	Henry is born
1470	Edward IV (York) Henry VI (Lancaster)	Lancastrians take back the Crown	Raglan	Henry freed and joins Jasper
1461	Henry VI (Lancaster) Edward IV (York)	Yorkists take the Crown	Pembroke and Raglan	_____
1471	Henry VI (Lancaster) Edward IV (York)	Battle of Tewkesbury	Pembroke and then _____	Henry flees with Jasper

Think!
Why did Henry Tudor invade Wales and England?

Read the list of reasons below and put them in order of priority, that is, the most important reasons first. Use the information from the story about Henry Tudor's early life.

- He wanted to become the King of England.
- He wanted to free Wales from English rule.
- He wanted revenge for the deaths of his father and his grandfather.
- He wanted revenge because of the years he had spent as a prisoner and as an exile.
- He was encouraged to invade by the King of France.
- He was encouraged to invade by members of the Yorkist family who hated Richard III because it was thought that Richard had murdered the Princes in the Tower.

Discuss your answers with other members of the class. There is not a right or wrong answer, since we do not know exactly what was in Henry Tudor's mind.

The march on Bosworth Field

Henry and his fleet sailed from France to the coast of Pembrokeshire. On 7 August they sailed into Milford Sound and landed in Mill Bay near Dale. Henry had returned to Wales. He was close to the castle where he was born and to the place from which he had escaped fourteen years before.

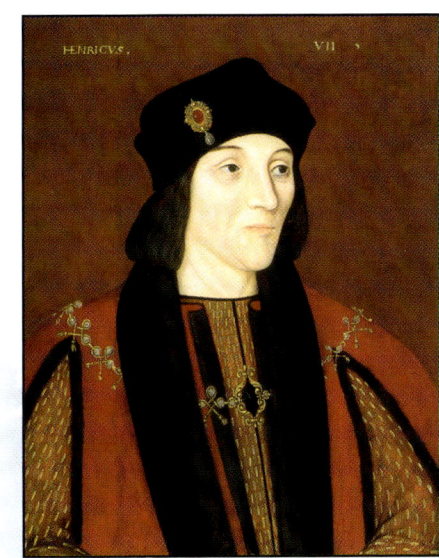

Henry VII, painted in about 1500.

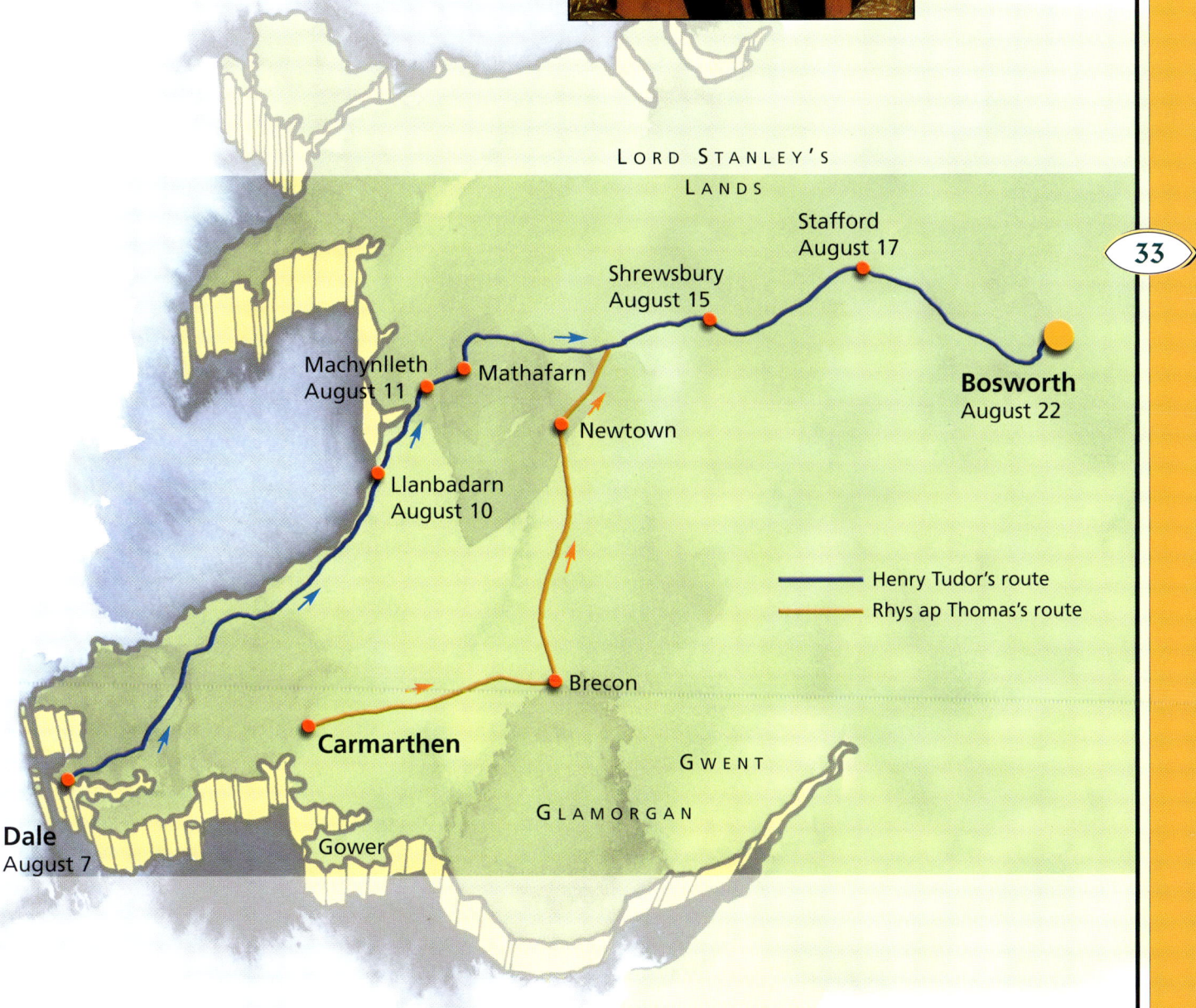

Map locations:
- Dale — August 7
- Llanbadarn — August 10
- Machynlleth — August 11
- Mathafarn
- Newtown
- Shrewsbury — August 15
- Stafford — August 17
- Bosworth — August 22
- Carmarthen
- Brecon
- Gower, Glamorgan, Gwent
- Lord Stanley's Lands

— Henry Tudor's route
— Rhys ap Thomas's route

Why did Henry choose to attack King Richard III by marching through Wales?

Henry's uncle, Jasper, had once been the duke of Pembroke.

Supporters of Richard III controlled the Gower, Glamorgan and Gwent.

Henry had been in contact with Lord Stanley and his brother Sir William Stanley. By then Lord Stanley was married to Henry's mother, Margaret Beaufort. He had lands and support in Cheshire and Lancashire. Sir William was King Richard III's representative in north Wales. Henry may have made an arrangement to meet the Stanleys at Shrewsbury.

Henry was also friendly with Rhys ap Thomas. Rhys was powerful in the area around Carmarthen. He had 2,000 men. His family had become strong through the support of the Lancastrian family. When Henry landed he made for Haverfordwest. Here, however, he received news that Rhys could not be trusted.

Think!

1. Why did Henry decide to land in Pembrokeshire?

2. Why did Henry march north from Pembrokeshire following a route along the west coast rather than other possible routes?

3. Why did Henry expect Sir William Stanley to support him even though he was Richard III's representative in north Wales?

4. Think about Rhys ap Thomas's position. Why might he have hesitated to join Henry?

TASK

Discuss these questions with a partner or as a class and copy out and complete the writing frame below.

I think that Henry VII landed in Pembrokeshire because . . .

One reason why Henry chose to march north via the west coast of Wales was . . .

Another reason is . . .

A further reason is . . .

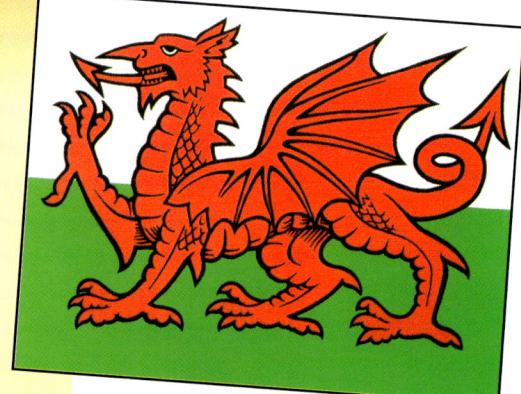

A Welshman claims the Crown

When Henry landed in Wales his supporters claimed that he was the 'Mab Darogan', the 'son of prophecy'. The Welsh bards or poets had been writing since the time of Owain Glyndŵr about the coming of a saviour to free Wales from English rule. His supporters also said that he was the true heir to the throne because he was descended on his father's side from a seventh-century British king called Cadwaladr. Henry's standard-bearer carried Cadwaladr's emblem on his flag – the red dragon on a green and white background. Today this is the national flag of Wales.

When Henry's red dragon was carried on Bosworth Field, it measured 8.1 metres (27 feet). How does this compare with the length of your classroom?

Dafydd Llwyd of Mathafarn

Henry's army marched up the west coast of Wales. One night during the march Henry stayed at Dafydd Llwyd's house at Mathafarn (see the map of Henry's journey). Dafydd was one of the most famous Welsh bards at this time. He also had a reputation as a prophet who could tell the future. Henry, it is said, asked Dafydd whether he would be successful against Richard III or not. Dafydd asked for time to think about his answer. During the night he talked to his wife. She advised him to tell Henry that he would win.

Can you think why Dafydd's wife gave this advice?

A modern photograph of Mathafarn.

If Henry won, Dafydd would be regarded as a prophet and might be rewarded. If Henry lost, he might be killed or would have been unlikely to come to Mathafarn again.

Key word

standard-bearer: person carrying the flag of the leader

Rhys ap Thomas

While Henry's army marched up the west coast of Wales, Rhys ap Thomas marched from his home at Dinefwr (see page 20) through the centre of Wales. At Machynlleth Henry decided to go east through the mountains to Welshpool. This was the most difficult part of the journey. Henry finally met Rhys on Long Mountain overlooking Welshpool. Rhys agreed to support Henry.

Key word

hostage: a person taken prisoner by one side in order to put pressure on the other side.

The Stanleys

Henry's army marched on to Shrewsbury. Men from Gwynedd joined him. Henry was expecting to meet with the Stanleys here, but they did not appear. King Richard III had seized Lord Stanley's son and held him hostage.

A later painting of the old Welsh Gate at Shrewsbury. Henry entered the town through this gate.

The two armies get closer

Richard's army of about 10,000 men marched to Market Bosworth in Leicestershire. Henry, who had about 7,000 men, marched towards him. The Stanleys had 3,000 men and arrived at the battlefield separately. The Stanleys still did not know who to support; after all, Lord Stanley's son was still being held hostage by King Richard.

Can you find Richard and his crown?

The Battle of Bosworth Field

The two armies started to fight at midday on 22 August. Richard had more soldiers than Henry. Henry, with a small group of soldiers, was cut off from the main battle. Richard saw this and decided that the quickest way to end the battle was to kill Henry. He attacked, leading his men himself. Henry was outnumbered. His bodyguards fought bravely but his standard-bearer was killed. At this point Sir William Stanley, who had stood back and watched the two armies fighting, made the decision to support Henry.

In the nick of time Sir William Stanley and his men came to Henry's rescue. Richard's troops scattered and left Richard fighting alone. Legend has it that Richard refused to escape on a horse and declared that he would 'die like a king, or win victory'. He was killed.

Henry Tudor becomes king

Henry's troops shouted 'God Save King Henry, God Save King Henry'. The story is told that Richard's crown was found under a thornbush. Lord Stanley took it and placed it on his stepson's head. King Henry VII was the last king of England to win the crown in battle, by killing the previous king.

What do you think this picture shows?

Think!

1. Why did the Stanleys delay in giving support to Henry and arrive at the battle as a separate army?

2. Why might the Stanleys think it was better to support Henry, rather than Richard? (There are no right or wrong answers to these questions. You, like any historian, can only suggest ideas from the evidence.)

3. Why could Henry Tudor be called lucky?

TASK

Imagine that you have to interview Henry after the Battle of Bosworth. Prepare a list of questions for the interview. Think about the time before the battle, the battle itself and the future. Put a member of the class in the 'hot seat' in the role of Henry VII and ask him or her your questions.

Henry VII and England

Key words
dynasty: a succession of rulers of the same family
monarchs: kings and queens

The gold medal produced to celebrate the marriage of Henry VII and Elizabeth of York in 1486.

Why did Henry VII make this rose the symbol of his family?

Many historians believe that Henry was a very important king of England. He helped England to become a strong and powerful country in the sixteenth century.

- He ruled for twenty-four years. He defeated all his enemies and the last twelve years of his reign were peaceful.

- He ended the fighting between Yorkists and Lancastrians.

- He married Elizabeth of York to bring both families together.

- He made changes to the law courts and improved law and order.

- He made the Crown rich again.

- He encouraged voyages to North America which began a new age of discovery.

- He arranged marriages for his children with other royal families in Europe, and other countries believed that England was powerful again.

- The Tudor dynasty kept the peace and ruled for over 100 years.

- His son, Henry VIII, and granddaughter, Elizabeth I, are two of the most famous monarchs in English history. They built on his achievements.

Henry VII is remembered as a strong English king, but what did he do for Wales?

Key words

court: a law court to hold trials but also means the place where a ruler lives and keeps his/her servants and followers, and the place of government, e.g. the English court
bishop: a leader of the Church
Yeomen of the Guard: the king's personal bodyguards

A large number of Welshmen had supported Henry at Bosworth, and their support had brought victory. His Welsh supporters saw him as a Welshman who had become King. They now expected rewards for their support.

What Henry did for the Welsh

- Welsh soldiers who had fought at Bosworth became his Yeomen of the Guard.

- The red dragon on a white and green background became one of his emblems.

- He named his first son Arthur, after the legendary king.

- He brought a Welsh harpist to the English court.

- He celebrated St David's Day at the English court.

- He rewarded Jasper Tudor.

- He rewarded Rhys ap Thomas.

- He rewarded Sir William Stanley by giving him many lands and official positions.

- Welshmen were appointed as bishops in Wales.

- Between 1505 and 1508 he got rid of the old anti-Welsh laws in some parts of north-east Wales (twenty years after he became king).

- Many Welshmen left Wales for London to get jobs in the King's court and to seek their fortune.

- In 1501 he set up a court at Ludlow to begin to deal with problems of law and order in Wales and on the border.

This is what one historian, C. S. Davies, has written about Henry and Wales:

Once he became king, Henry had no reason to please the Welsh. Little was done for the Welsh people, although numbers of individual Welshmen made a career for themselves at court.

Think!

1. Read through the things that Henry did as king. Why did Henry do these things? Who was he trying to please? Which things did he do to help the people of Wales? Which things did he do to make himself a strong king of England?

2. Read the quotation by C. S. Davies. What evidence would you give in support of the statement and what evidence would you give against?

Was Henry VII good for Wales or not?

Key words
feuds: quarrels, often fighting, over long periods of time
raids: sudden attacks

Read the following descriptions of Wales in the 1530s:

- *Feuds, murders, organized raids on towns, cattle-stealing, kidnapping, attacks on merchants and piracy were some, but not all, of the list of disorderly activities.*

- *The lives of the 50 per cent or more of families who were the poorest farmers, cottagers and labourers, was still very harsh.*

- *When John Leland visited Wales he found little that was positive to say about the towns he visited: 'by English standards they were small, many were in decay and the inhabitants poor.'*

What impression do these accounts give of early Tudor Wales?

What impression is given about Henry VII's impact on Wales?

On the other hand, George Owen, a rich landowner living at the end of the century, considered Henry to have been good for Wales. Owen was a member of the gentry class.

The gentry were the richest people in Wales. They made up about 5 per cent of the population. They owned the land and lived in fine houses. In the hundred years after Henry VII came to the throne they became even more wealthy. Many married into English families.

Once Henry had become king many ambitious Welshmen headed for London. Some got positions at court and others became involved in trade and business. Henry's Welsh connections made it fashionable to be Welsh. Many Welsh gentry made themselves rich and used their money to buy land in Wales.

London in 1600. Looking at the picture, can you suggest reasons why Welsh people wanted to go to London?

The Acts of Union

Key words

Parliament: the law-making body of government, at that time made up of the king with representatives of the landowning classes

In the reign of Henry VIII, Henry VII's son, the English Parliament passed laws which were known as the Acts of Union. As a result the gentry in Wales were put in charge of collecting taxes and of keeping the peace. For the first time Wales elected Members of Parliament to go and sit in the English Parliament. The MPs were members of the Welsh gentry. As well as being rich, the gentry were by this time the most powerful people in Wales.

Think!

In 1602 George Owen wrote a book in which he said that Henry VII was a great leader who had helped the people of Wales. At that time, Henry's granddaughter Elizabeth was on the throne.

- Who would be able to read what he wrote?
- What lifestyles did he and fellow members of the gentry have?
- Why do you think that George Owen had such a good opinion of Henry Tudor?
- What type of people might disagree with George Owen's opinion?

Sir Christopher Vaughan of Tretower, a member of the Welsh gentry. How does the picture show that the gentry were rich and powerful?

TURNING POINT

At the start of this chapter you were asked to consider if Henry's reign was a turning point in the history of Wales. This is not very easy because there are different points of view about Henry VII and his achievements.

It has been said that there was a lot of disappointment in Wales with Henry. On the other hand a lot of individual Welshmen did very well for themselves. Henry's reign was a 'turning point' for some people in Wales, but for others there was very little change. If they were poor, life went on in the same way.

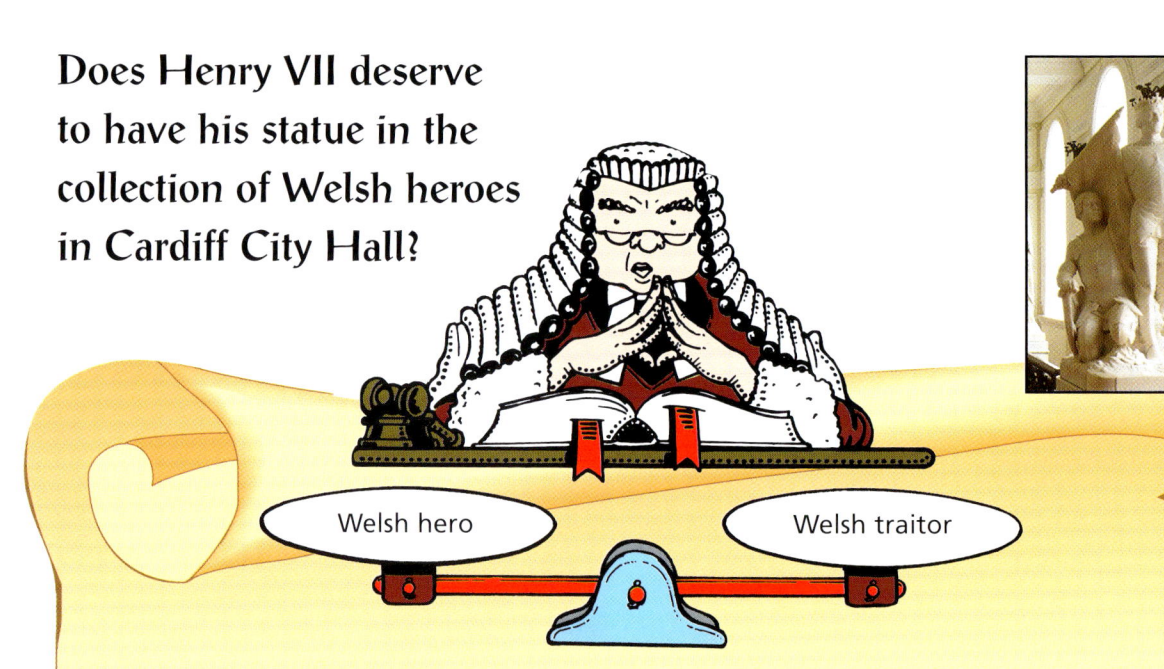

Does Henry VII deserve to have his statue in the collection of Welsh heroes in Cardiff City Hall?

Welsh hero — **Welsh traitor**

TASK

Look at the list of statements. Some support the case for Henry's statue remaining in the collection of Welsh heroes and some help the case against.

Discuss the statements with a partner and put them into two groups – one group in favour and one group against.

- Henry was a Welshman who became king of England.
- Henry was mainly concerned with making sure that he kept his throne and that the Crown was wealthy.
- Henry's supporters, many of them Welshmen, became richer and more powerful after he became king.
- It is true that Henry rewarded his supporters well, but he did nothing for the majority of people in Wales.
- After 1485, Henry never returned to Wales.
- One hundred years after Henry's death Wales was controlled by the gentry class who were from Welsh families.
- At the end of his reign the anti-Welsh laws, passed at the time of Owain Glyndŵr's rebellion, were still in the lawbooks in most parts of Wales.
- The gentry lived in fine new houses. They did not have to live in fortified castles to protect themselves.
- The people of Wales were loyal to the Tudors. There were revolts in Cornwall, the north of England and Ireland, but none in Wales.
- Henry was a great soldier. His victory at Bosworth Field, with a third of his army being Welsh, reflected glory on Wales as well as on himself.
- He did nothing to support the Welsh language. During his reign ambitious people thought it was important to learn English as this would help them to get better jobs and positions with the government.

Judgement time!

Now it is time to decide what you think. Using the evidence above and any more points that you can think of, write a paragraph supporting one side or the other.

What does your class think?

Discuss the points with your teacher and then take a vote. Will your class vote for Henry's statue to remain in Cardiff City Hall or are you going to write to Cardiff County Council and ask them to take it away?

1.3 Why was the translation of the Bible into Welsh in 1588 an important event in Welsh history?

Key word

bilingual: speaking two languages

Your enquiry

In this enquiry you will work out why it was important to translate the Bible into Welsh in 1588. The translation of the Bible into Welsh was a major reason why the Welsh language was able to survive and therefore helps to explain why Wales is a bilingual country today.

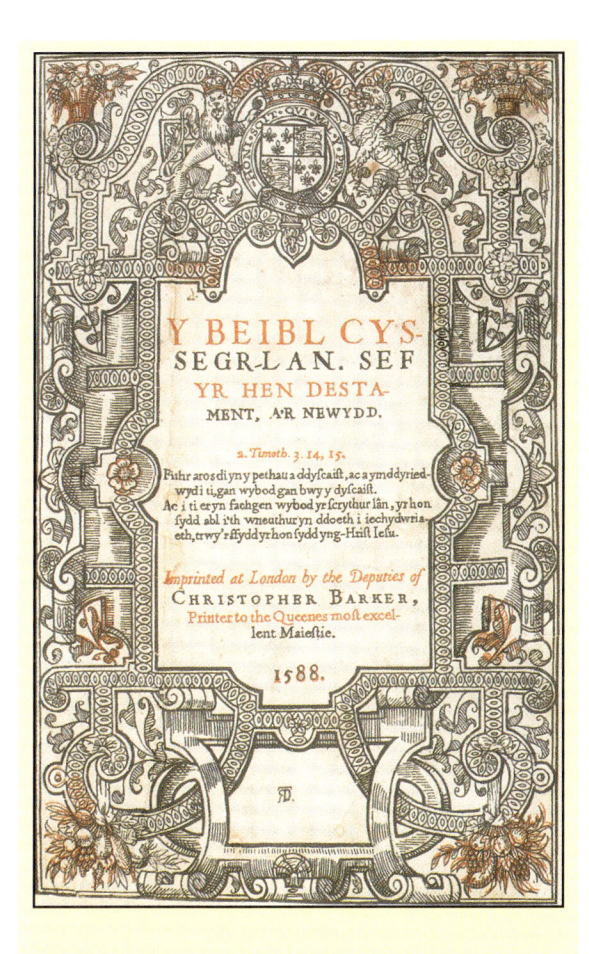

Today, one thing that makes Wales different from other parts of the British Isles is the fact that it is a **bilingual** country. Both Welsh and English are spoken, written and read.

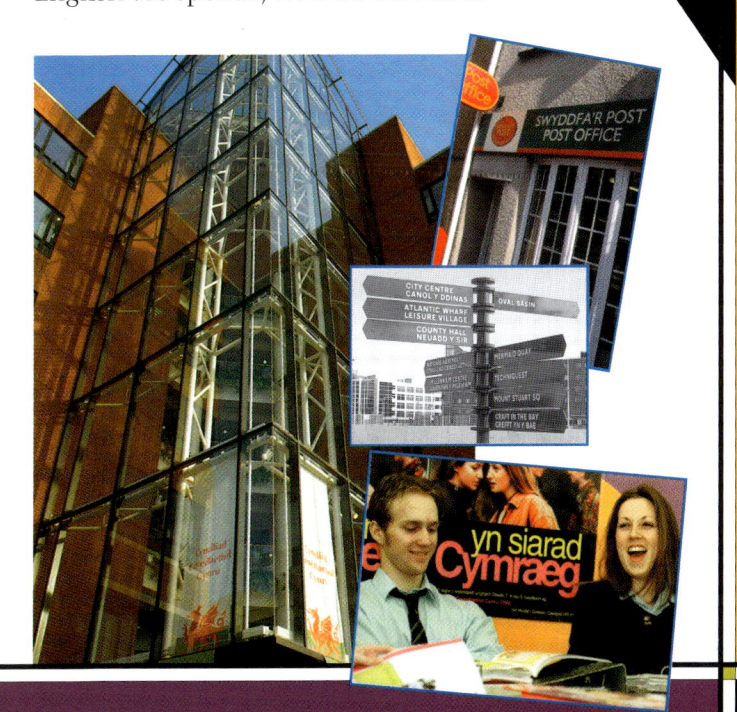

This is the front page of the first complete Bible in the Welsh language. It was translated into Welsh by William Morgan.

Looking at the illustration, find the answers to these questions:
- When was it published?
- Where was it printed?
- Do you know who the Queen was then?
- Do you think the Queen thought that printing the Bible in Welsh was a good idea?

Catholics and Protestants

The Reformation in Europe in the sixteenth century

Key words

Reformation: sixteenth-century movement to reform the Catholic Church which ended in the Protestants breaking away from the Catholic Church
relics: bones of a holy person
pilgrimage: journey to a holy place
mass: Catholic church service

To help you understand about the reasons for the translation of the Bible into Welsh you need to know about religion in the sixteenth century.

At the start of the sixteenth century there was only one Christian Church. It was called the Catholic Church. Its leader was the Pope who lived in Rome.

In 1517 a German monk called Martin Luther criticized the Catholic Church and the Pope. He was supported by some powerful German princes. Luther's supporters became known as Protestants.

The differences between...

CATHOLICS AND PROTESTANTS

The **Pope in Rome was head of the Catholic Church**. He was God's representative on earth.

Protestants **did not accept the Pope as head of the church**. In some Protestant countries the rulers made themselves head of the church, for example, Henry VIII in England and Wales.

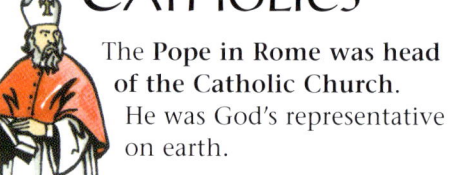

Catholic believers were **helped by the priests to communicate with God**. They also prayed to saints to ask them to speak to God on their behalf. Sometimes they went on pilgrimages to visit saints' relics.

Protestants believed that it was possible for **everyone to speak directly to God** when they prayed.

Catholics believed what they were told by the **Church and its clergy** (that is, the Pope, bishops, priests and monks).

Protestants said that people should only believe **what was written in the Bible**.

Catholic services were **in Latin**.

Protestants believed that the Bible and church services should be in the **language of the believers**.

During the most important church service, the mass, Catholics believe that **a miracle** takes place when the bread and wine becomes the body and blood of Jesus.

Protestants believe that the taking of the bread and wine is a way of **remembering** Jesus. The bread and wine do not change into His body and blood.

Catholic churches were **highly decorated** in praise of God and Jesus.

Many Protestant churches were **quite bare**. Some Protestants destroyed statues in Catholic churches and whitewashed the walls to cover up the paintings. Some Protestants were against the use of music in churches.

Key words

confess sins: tell a Catholic priest what you have done wrong
soul: moral, religious part of a human being

Understanding Catholic and Protestant beliefs in the sixteenth century

I am a Catholic

I am a Protestant

Henry VIII has no right to make himself the head of the Church. The Pope is chosen by God to be our leader on earth.

Now that pilgrimages to the cathedral have been banned, how will I get St David's support for my mother to go to heaven?

I haven't read anything in the Bible that says we have to go to church and confess our sins to the priest.

It is difficult for us today to understand everything that was important to people living in the past. We must remember that in the sixteenth century in western Europe everyone was a Christian. They believed then that their aim in life was to go to heaven when they died. Catholics and Protestants believed that there were different ways of getting there.

I've heard that the people who are reading the Bible for themselves are quarrelling. They can't agree on the meaning.

TASK

Read about the differences between Catholics and Protestants again and then discuss these statements with a partner. Which of the statements do you think would have been spoken by a Catholic and which by a Protestant?

I like the old Latin services. We all know what to sing and the priest speaks to God on our behalf.

Now that Queen Elizabeth has banned the mass, what chance do we have that our souls will go to heaven?

I find it very comforting to know that God hears my prayers when I speak to him at night.

When people are singing they don't listen to the words properly. It is the words that are most important.

Protestant changes in Wales

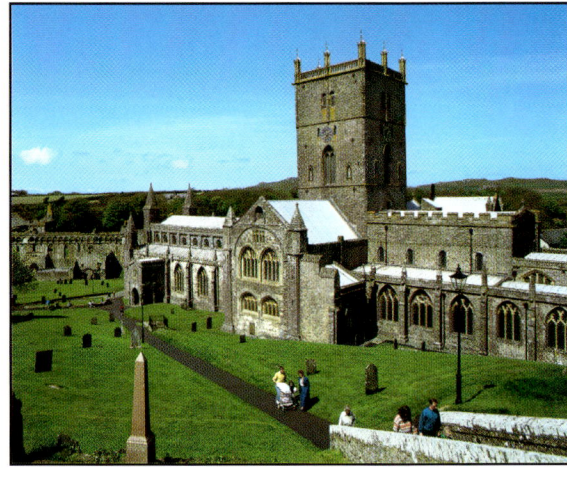

Key word

shrine: place of worship where saint's relics are kept

Before the 1530s, everyone in England and Wales was Catholic and went to church every Sunday. Villagers were often proud of their local church. Inside there were beautiful things which they could not afford for themselves, such as gold and silver crosses, paintings on the walls, gold candlesticks and colourful stained-glass windows. Some churches had shrines with the bones of saints (relics). These were important because Catholics believed that praying at a shrine meant that the saint would take their side in heaven. The most important shrine in Wales was at St David's Cathedral, where the bones of St David himself were said to be found.

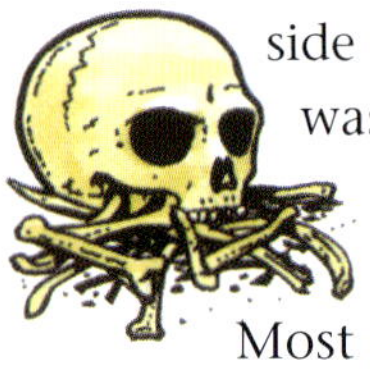

Most people believed in heaven and hell. Going to church regularly would help them get to heaven when they died. Although the language of the Catholic services was in Latin, people were familiar with the service. They knew when to reply to the priest, when to stand, sit or kneel.

Under King Henry VIII, the Church in England and Wales split away from the Catholic Church and became 'Protestant', with Henry as head of the Church instead of the Pope. When Henry died, his young son Edward became King and made more Protestant changes.

This is a modern reproduction of the statue of the Virgin Mary at Penrhys, Rhondda, which was burned by Protestants.

Protestant changes under Edward VI (1547–1553)

- Churches were raided and pictures and ornaments were destroyed or stolen.
- Walls were whitewashed (to cover pictures on the walls).
  - Statues and shrines were destroyed.
  - Pilgrimages were banned.
  - Priests and monks were allowed to get married.
  - The Bible in English was used in church.
  - English became the language of church services.

But most people in Wales spoke Welsh and did not understand English. These changes were not welcome. There was no serious rebellion in Wales, though in Cornwall, where most of the population spoke Cornish at that time, there was a revolt lasting a year which was put down harshly.

TASK

Read the list of changes made under King Edward VI. Explain why they were disliked by many people in Wales.

The Catholics return for only five years

The burning of a Protestant martyr, Anne Askew, in England.

Key word

martyr: someone put to death for his/her beliefs

When Edward VI died in 1553, his elder sister Mary became Queen. She brought back the Catholic Church.

- Church services were again made Catholic and everyone had to go to church every Sunday.
- Church services were in Latin. In Wales many people were happy to see the return of the old familiar Catholic services.
- Priests could not marry.
- Those who refused to accept the Catholic Church were to be burned at the stake. There were three Protestant martyrs in Wales. In England there were 281.

Mary became ill and died in 1558. Her younger sister Elizabeth then became Queen Elizabeth I.

This picture shows the torture of a Protestant by the Catholic government of Queen Mary, but Elizabeth's government later used similar methods to torture Catholics.

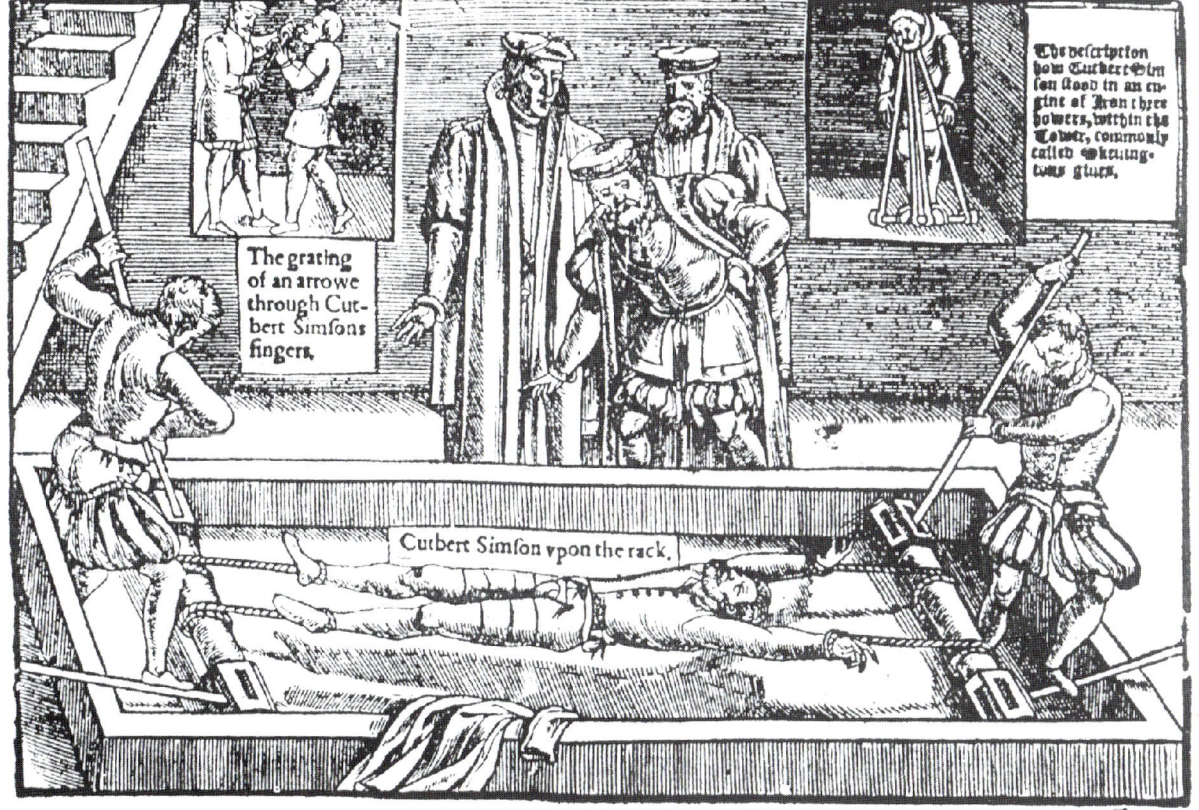

In **Scotland**, Elizabeth's Catholic cousin was Queen (Mary, Queen of Scots), but many Protestants were unhappy with her rule.

The English government claimed to rule **Ireland**. They only firmly controlled the area around Dublin. Most of the Irish were Catholics.

When Queen Elizabeth became Queen of **England** in 1558, England and Wales became Protestant again. England and Wales first became Protestant during the reign of Elizabeth's father Henry VIII (1534–1547) and during the reign of her brother Edward (1547–1553). Her sister Mary Tudor had made the country Catholic again (1553–1558).

The official religion in **Wales** was the same as that in England. Most people, however, did not like the new Protestant services because they were held in English and they only understood Welsh.

Spain was the most powerful Catholic country in Europe. Protestants had been almost wiped out there.

LONDON

PARIS

France was a Catholic country. However, the Protestants were a powerful group and for most of Elizabeth's reign, the French Protestants and Catholics were fighting each other.

Philip II, King of **Spain**, had married Mary Tudor. When Mary died in 1588, Philip wanted to keep control of England by marrying Mary's younger sister Elizabeth. Elizabeth refused.

LISBON

CADIZ

TASK

Make a list of countries that had Protestant leaders in 1558, when Elizabeth became Queen, and those that had Catholic leaders. In which countries do you think there was fighting between Protestants and Catholics?

Key
- Protestant
- Catholic

Europe in 1558

In the years that followed Martin Luther's attack on the Catholic Church, there were civil wars in many European countries between the supporters of the old Catholic Church and the new Protestant believers. By the time Elizabeth I became Queen of England in 1558 this was the situation in Europe.

Large parts of **Germany** were Protestant. Germany at this time was divided into a large number of small states.

Spain ruled the countries we know today as **Belgium** and **the Netherlands**. The Protestants in the Netherlands protested against the Catholic government in Spain.

The Pope remained head of the Catholic Church, based in Rome. **Italy** was divided into a number of small states.

ROME

This map has been adapted to make pupils more aware of geographical regions.

PROTESTANT | CATHOLIC

Think! Can you explain this diagram to a partner?

Elizabeth makes the Church Protestant again

When Elizabeth became Queen, the Church became Protestant again, but not as extreme as the Protestantism of Edward.

- Protestant church services were brought back and everyone had to go to Protestant church services every Sunday.
- Church services were in English again.
- The Bible in English replaced the Bible in Latin in all churches.
- Priests were again allowed to marry.
- The Prayer Book was changed so that it was less Protestant than it had been under Edward.

Elizabeth's government knew, however, that Protestant changes had been unpopular in Wales in particular during Edward's reign, and they were afraid that dislike of Protestant church services in English might turn the Welsh against the government.

- The government got Parliament to pass a law in 1563 ordering the translation of the Prayer Book and Bible into Welsh.
- By the early 1580s the translation of the Bible into Welsh had still not been completed. Welsh Protestants believed that the Church was not doing enough to encourage the new religion in Wales.
- The 1580s were a dangerous time. Protestant England was moving towards war against Catholic Spain. Would the Welsh people be loyal to the Queen, especially as the changes promised in 1563 had still not taken place?

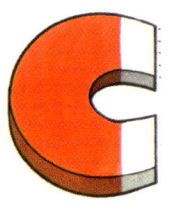

Information and tasks on the following pages will help you to understand why the 1580s were a dangerous time.

TASK

A.

Sort the statements on pages 52 and 53 into three sets based on events in

1. Spain and the Netherlands;
2. England; and
3. Wales.

Events in Spain and the Netherlands
1558–1588

Events in England
1558–1588

Events in Wales
1558–1588

B.

Once you have sorted the events under these headings, arrange them in chronological order.

C.
Questions on statements.

1. Look at the events about Spain and the Netherlands.
   a) What did Spain do in 1571 and 1580?
   b) How do these events help to explain why the Spanish were feared in England and Wales?
   c) Look back at the map. Why was the English government afraid that Spain had large numbers of soldiers in the Netherlands?
   d) Find three reasons that Philip of Spain could give to explain why he was invading England and Wales in 1588.

2. Look at events in England.
   a) Who did Catholics in England and Wales want to be Queen instead of Elizabeth?
   b) How did the Catholics threaten Elizabeth in these years?
   c) Why do you think that Elizabeth had her cousin, Mary, Queen of Scots, executed?

3. Look at events in or about Wales.
   a) Why was Queen Elizabeth's Council worried about Wales in the 1580s?
   b) What was William Morgan's task?

D.

Look at the pictures on pages 54 and 55, and read what is written there. You will then have more detailed information about events in 1587. Can you work out a connection between the events described? Write a paragraph to explain your ideas.

Events in Spain, the Netherlands, England and Wales

These pages are designed for use as a card-sorting exercise. They should be photocopied and made up into cards.

1558-1588

1586
(August) The Spanish Ambassador in London wrote to the King of Spain telling him that the people of Wales 'are much attached to the Catholic religion and the Queen of Scotland'.

1588
(May) The Spanish Armada (134 ships) left Spain to invade England and Wales.

1559
The English Parliament passed laws to make England a Protestant country again.

1563
(April) The Act for the translation of the Bible into Welsh was passed following the concern of Welsh bishops that the people of Wales could not understand the Protestant church services which were carried out in English.

1566
The Dutch revolt against Spain began.

1578
William Morgan, vicar at Llanrhaeadr-ym-Mochnant, began his work on translating the Bible into Welsh.

1586
(May) Queen Elizabeth's Privy Council was worried about the lack of enthusiasm for the Protestant religion in Wales and about illegal meetings of Catholics there.

1571
The Spanish won a major victory at sea in the Mediterranean against the Turks.

1588
The Welsh translation of the Bible was published.

1568
Mary, Queen of Scots escaped from prison in Scotland. She fled to England. Elizabeth imprisoned the woman who was her Catholic rival for the throne.

1588
(July) The Spanish Armada arrived in English waters at the end of the month. It failed to land. Out of 130 ships only 60 returned to Spain. Nearly 19,000 men died.

1580
Spain took over Portugal.

1587
William Morgan spent most of the year in London preparing the Welsh Bible for publication.

1587
(February) A secret Catholic printing press was found in a cave on the Little Orme, near Llandudno.

1569
The Northern Rebellion broke out. This was a major Catholic rebellion against Queen Elizabeth.

1587
(April) Sir Francis Drake destroyed 30 Spanish ships in the port of Cadiz, southern Spain.

1585
Queen Elizabeth sent an army to support the Dutch who were fighting against Spanish rule of the Netherlands.

1571–1586
A number of Catholic plots against Elizabeth and three assassination attempts.

1587
(February) Philip of Spain and other Catholic leaders condemned the execution of Mary, Queen of Scots.

1587
(February) Mary, Queen of Scots was executed, accused of supporting plots against Elizabeth.

This picture shows the execution of the Catholic Mary, Queen of Scots, in February 1587. She had been accused of plotting to kill her cousin, the Protestant Queen of England and Wales, Queen Elizabeth I.

Events in
1587

All these events took place in 1587. They are all closely connected.

Protestant England and Wales quarrelled with Catholic Spain throughout Elizabeth I's reign from 1558 to 1603. In 1587, Philip II, the King of Spain, planned to invade England and Wales. In April 1587, Sir Francis Drake, an English sea captain, attacked first. His fleet sank 30 Spanish ships in the port of Cadiz.

During Elizabeth's reign, it was against the law for Catholics to attend their own religious services. Catholic priests, however, came into England and Wales and held secret services. Elizabeth and her ministers were concerned that, if Spain invaded England and Wales, people who still believed in the Catholic Church would support the Spanish invaders. In February 1587 it was discovered that a cave on the Little Orme, near Llandudno, had been used to hide Catholic priests and to print Catholic books.

'In the county of Caernarfon . . . there is a cave by the sea side the haunt of Catholic priests in these parts. They were discovered by a neighbour who saw at the cave mouth one or two of them with pistol whom he spake with and found them strangers . . . There was found the next day in the cave weapons, food and an altar . . .'

Adapted from a letter from William Griffith, JP, to Archbishop Whitgift, on 19 April 1587. It was at this cave that a secret printing press was discovered; it was secret because it was illegal to print Catholic books or pamphlets at that time.

Events in 1587

One of the purposes of your enquiry is to find out **WHY?**

This picture shows the kind of printing workshop where the Welsh Protestant vicar William Morgan would have worked in London during 1587. He was in charge of the printing of the Bible into Welsh. The Archbishop of Canterbury, John Whitgift, ordered Morgan to come to London to make sure the Welsh Bible was published.

Why was Wales important to Queen Elizabeth's government?

Information on the next three pages will provide more detail about events in Wales. This will help you understand why the translation of the Bible into Welsh was so important.

Wales is surrounded by sea on three sides. The best ports were thought to be on Anglesey and at Milford Haven.

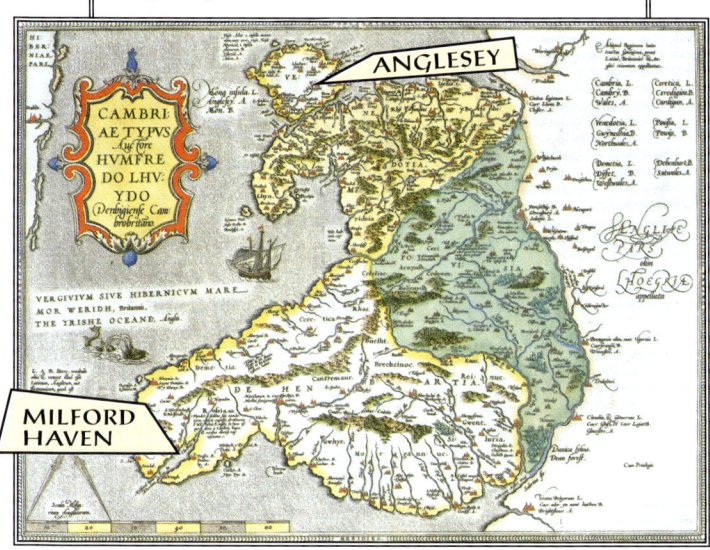

The year 1587 was a dangerous time for Queen Elizabeth. Mary, Queen of Scots, her Catholic cousin, was executed. This angered Spain, the most powerful Catholic country in Europe. War between the two countries threatened. At this time of great danger John Whitgift, the Archbishop of Canterbury, ordered William Morgan, vicar of Llanrhaeadr-ym-Mochnant, to come to London to supervise the printing of the Welsh Bible. **Why was publication so important in 1587?**

The population of Wales in 1550 was approximately 225,000. Most people lived in small villages and settlements. A small number of people lived in towns. The largest town was Carmarthen with a population of just over 2,000.

Bernardino de Mendoza, the Spanish ambassador to the English Court, described Wales in 1586:

> 'In South and North Wales the land is rather mountainous but the country is rich in sheep and cattle. There is plenty of wheat and the ports are numerous and good.'

Wales was close to Ireland. Elizabeth's government had difficulty in controlling Ireland. Protestant ideas were unpopular there and Irish rebels might be happy to support Spain. Ireland could provide a good base from which to attack England and Wales.

Morys Clynnog, a Catholic exile living in Rome, had drawn up an invasion plan for the Pope in 1575. He reminded him that Elizabeth's grandfather, Henry VII, had once led a successful invasion after landing in Wales.

Think!

Philip, the King of Spain, was planning to invade England and Wales. Using the information on the page, give reasons for and against landing the Spanish army in Wales.

Copy out the table below with your ideas.

Reasons for King Philip II of Spain to land an invasion army in Wales

1 _____
2 _____
3 _____

Reasons against landing an invasion army in Wales

1 _____
2 _____
3 _____

Law and order in Wales

Key words

outlaw: wanted by the law
sheriff: official appointed to keep law and order

Piracy off the coasts of Wales was common. In 1569 it was claimed that pirates had a base on Bardsey Island. They were working with the local people of Caernarfonshire who took the stolen goods to sell in the fairs and markets of Chester. Government officials such as Edward Kemys of Glamorgan, who was a sheriff, were often accused of being in league with pirates.

Wales had a reputation for being a wild and dangerous place in Tudor times.

In the 1530s, following reports that Wales was out of control, Henry VIII sent Rowland Lee to Wales to make sure that law-breakers were punished. It is said that Lee ordered 5,000 men to be hanged within six years.

In the 1550s a gang of outlaws, known as the Red Bandits of Mawddwy, 'robbed, burned and murdered' in the area around Cader Idris. In 1555 Lewis Owen, the sheriff of Merioneth, captured over 80 of the bandits in their hideout and had them hanged. In revenge, several months later, Lewis Owen was ambushed whilst travelling through the thick woods of Mawddwy on his way to the law courts in Montgomery.

Cefn Mabli, the house of Edward Kemys, in the sixteenth century

The Mawddwy valley

Think!

Why might the Queen's Council in London be concerned about the loyalty of the Welsh on hearing stories and reports like the ones above?

> *The outlaws cut down several long trees to impede his passage. Then they discharged a shower of arrows; one of which hit him in the face. He took it out . . . but after this they attacked him with pikes and javelins and left him dead with thirty wounds.*
> (Thomas Pennant, writing in 1784.)

TASK

Make a list of reasons why Elizabeth's Council might not trust the Welsh

_____
_____
_____
_____

Catholics in Wales in Elizabeth's time

- At the start of Elizabeth's reign, a number of Welsh Catholics escaped abroad because they knew that Elizabeth was a Protestant. Some trained to become priests.

- Welsh Catholic priests who had gone abroad began to return in disguise and live in hiding in the homes of people who were secretly Catholic.

A priest hole at Harvington Hall in England, near the Welsh border

- In 1584, a Catholic schoolteacher, Richard Gwyn, was executed at Wrexham. He was accused of organizing a network of undercover Catholic priests in north Wales. He was hanged, drawn and quartered – after hanging, he was disembowelled and his body then cut into four. His head and one quarter were taken to Denbigh castle and the other quarters were shown at Ruthin, Holt and Wrexham.

- Other Catholics set up a secret printing press in a cave on the Little Orme, near Llandudno. They lived there for six months and printed books in Welsh that explained Catholic teaching about the Bible. They were discovered in February 1587 but managed to escape.

- Hugh Owen, a Welsh Catholic, worked as a spy for King Philip II of Spain. Another Welshman, Thomas Morgan, lived in Paris and worked on behalf of Mary, Queen of Scots. Together with the Spanish ambassador in London, they encouraged Philip of Spain to believe that the people of Wales would rebel against Elizabeth and support the return of the Catholic Church.

- Thomas Morgan was involved in the Babington Plot in 1586. When this plot was discovered by the government, Anthony Babington, and several others including two Welsh gentlemen, were tortured for more information and then executed. Mary, Queen of Scots was then tried for plotting against Queen Elizabeth and executed.

Think!
1. Why did Queen Elizabeth's government treat Richard Gwyn so brutally?
2. How reliable do you think was the information given to the King of Spain by the Spanish ambassador and by Welsh Catholic spies like Hugh Owen?

TASK
More reasons why Elizabeth's Council might not trust the Welsh

_____
_____
_____
_____

A letter from the Archbishop of Canterbury

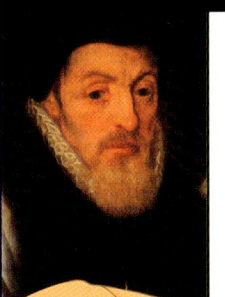

It is April 1587. You are Archbishop John Whitgift. You have ordered William Morgan to come to London to oversee the printing of the Bible into Welsh, which you have agreed to pay for. Write a letter to the Queen's Council explaining why you have taken these decisions. Use your notes to help you. Try to include key words that you have learnt, and refer to the glossary if you need to.

TASK

Since the execution of Mary, Queen of Scots, Philip of Spain is threatening to invade. I have reason to believe that he might land in Wales. It would be a good place for him to land because (see page 56) . . .
_____
_____
_____

He may get support from the people of Wales. They are not very trustworthy because (see page 57) . . .
_____
_____
_____

Furthermore the Protestant religion is not very popular in Wales because (see page 46) . . .
_____
_____
_____

There is also evidence of Catholic activity in Wales (see page 58) . . .
_____
_____
_____

We want the people of Wales to be loyal to the Queen and the government. If the Bible is translated into Welsh . . .
_____
_____
_____

What was the effect on Wales of having a Bible in Welsh?

We have looked at the reasons for the translation of the Bible into Welsh. But did it make any difference in Wales?

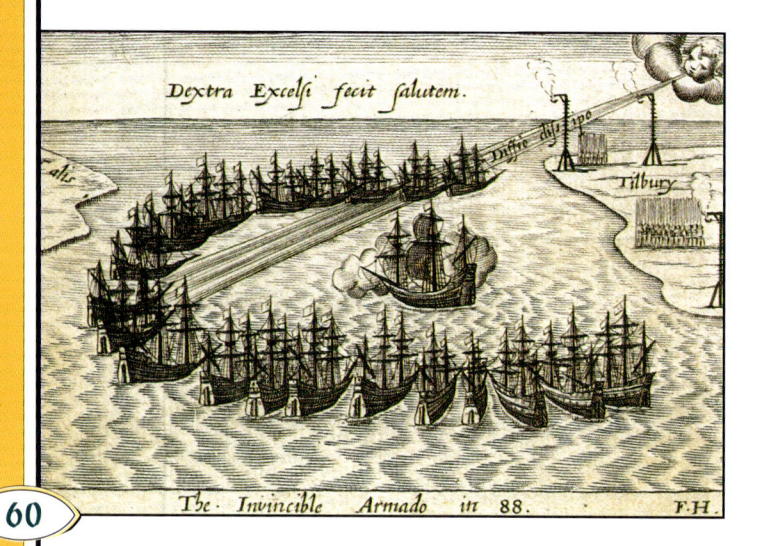

One of the far-reaching effects is still with us today. This is the existence in Wales of the Welsh language.

Let us return to the present day. Today:
The official language of Great Britain is English.
The official language of France is French.
The official language of Spain is Spanish.

But in all these countries, other languages are spoken by people whose ancestors have lived there for centuries.

In Great Britain, Welsh,
    Gaelic and Irish are spoken.
In France, Breton and
    Occitan are spoken.
In Spain, Catalan, Basque
    and Galician are spoken.

The year 1588 is one of the most famous dates in British history. It is the year of the Spanish Armada when the invasion attempt by the Spanish King Philip II was defeated.

Today, 20.5 per cent of the population of Wales speak Welsh. Welsh remains a strong language today, yet other languages which were equally as strong in the sixteenth century have either died out or are less widely spoken today.

However, this is what Professor Philip Jenkins has written:
'In Welsh history, it is the publication of a complete Bible in Welsh rather than the Armada which gives the year its real significance.'

A significant event is one that is very important and has far-reaching effects.

In the sixteenth century:
- the majority of people in Wales spoke Welsh.
- many people in Scotland spoke Gaelic.
- the majority of people in Ireland spoke Irish.
- the majority of people in Cornwall spoke Cornish.
- the majority of people in the Isle of Man spoke Manx.

Now read these statements below:

> In 1800 nearly 3 out of 4 people in Wales spoke Welsh.

> In Northern Ireland today there are more speakers of Chinese than there are speakers of Irish.

> The last native speaker of Manx died in 1974.

> The last native speaker of Cornish died in 1777.

> In Scotland approximately 15% of the population spoke Gaelic in the nineteenth century.

Key words

minority language: language spoken by fewer people than the main language of a country

Think!
What do these facts tell you about Welsh compared with these other languages?

Now think about this information:
The Bible was first published in Welsh in 1588.
The Bible was first published in Irish in 1690.
The Bible was first published in Scots Gaelic in 1801.
The Bible was never published in either Cornish or Manx.

What could you suggest about the importance of the translation of the Bible into Welsh from this information?

Look at the map:
1. What are the minority languages within the United Kingdom?
2. Identify France, Spain and Germany on the map and list their minority languages and the official language of the country.

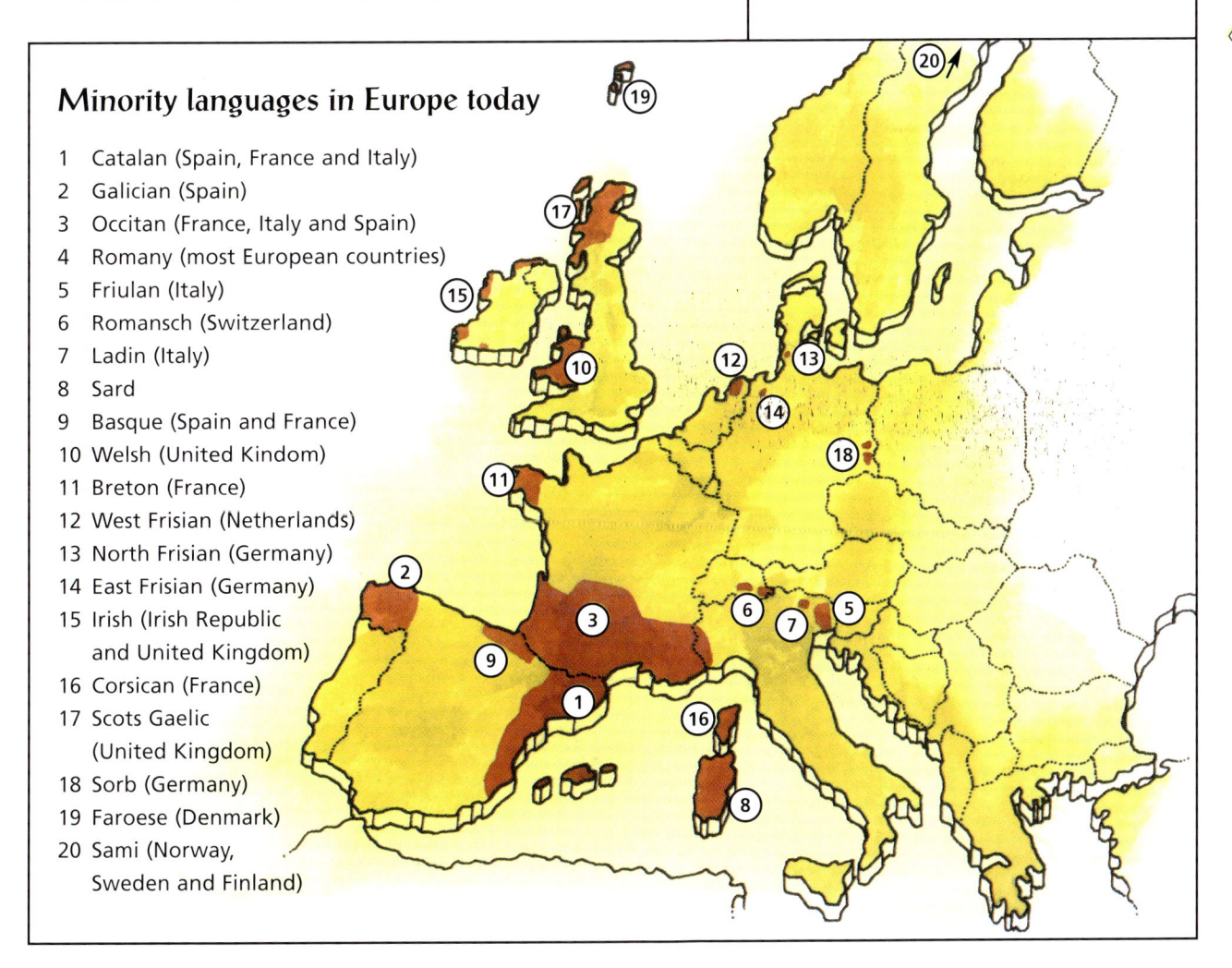

Minority languages in Europe today

1. Catalan (Spain, France and Italy)
2. Galician (Spain)
3. Occitan (France, Italy and Spain)
4. Romany (most European countries)
5. Friulan (Italy)
6. Romansch (Switzerland)
7. Ladin (Italy)
8. Sard
9. Basque (Spain and France)
10. Welsh (United Kindom)
11. Breton (France)
12. West Frisian (Netherlands)
13. North Frisian (Germany)
14. East Frisian (Germany)
15. Irish (Irish Republic and United Kingdom)
16. Corsican (France)
17. Scots Gaelic (United Kingdom)
18. Sorb (Germany)
19. Faroese (Denmark)
20. Sami (Norway, Sweden and Finland)

The Welsh language in the sixteenth century

The Welsh language was under threat in the sixteenth century.

1. Many of the Welsh gentry thought that if they spoke English it would help them to advance themselves, especially after Henry Tudor had become King. Then there were more opportunities for Welsh people to get work at the King's court and in London itself. Some Welsh gentry married into English families and sent their sons to English public schools.

2. When the Acts of Union between England and Wales were passed in 1536 and 1543, they stated that the language of the law courts had to be English. They also stated that all holders of official positions in Wales had to speak English. These laws affected mainly the ruling class. If members of the gentry wanted to get important jobs they had to speak English.

3. The ordinary people of Wales did not immediately see much change after the Acts of Union, but when King Edward VI (1547–1553) ordered the services in church to be carried out in English, this affected everyone greatly. Now that the law courts and churches used only English, the future of the Welsh language was threatened.

This statue of Sir Hugh Myddleton, who came originally from Ruthin, stands in Islington Green in London. Hugh was the son of a Welsh landowner and he made his fortune in London at the end of the sixteenth century as a goldsmith and also built a new freshwater system for London. His brother Thomas was also a wealthy merchant and became an MP and Lord Mayor of London.

Protestant leaders in Wales were very concerned, mainly because the people could not understand the new Protestant religion. 'The word of God', wrote William Salesbury, 'is being strangled.' If the people of Wales were to be converted to Protestantism the language of the church services needed to be in Welsh.

In 1563 the English Parliament was persuaded to pass an Act for the translation of the Bible into Welsh.

Twenty-five years later William Morgan, a Denbighshire vicar, completed the task. He took ten years himself and was able to build on the earlier work of William Salesbury who had already translated the New Testament in the 1560s.

Professor Glanmor Williams says that 'making Welsh the language of public worship made it more important and ensured its survival'.

You may wonder what difference it made to have a Bible in Welsh when most people still could not read. Remember that everyone had to go to church. They could now hear the stories of the Bible in their own language for the first time and could begin to understand the church services.

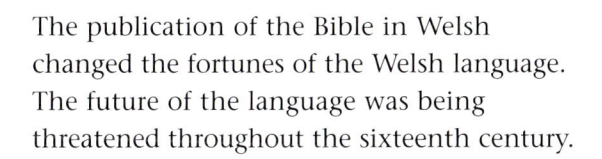

The publication of the Bible in Welsh changed the fortunes of the Welsh language. The future of the language was being threatened throughout the sixteenth century.

However, after the publication of the Bible in Welsh, Welsh was to remain the language of the majority of the people of Wales for the next 300 years.

The long-term results of having the Bible in Welsh

After 1588 the language of church services in Wales became Welsh. Even 160 years later, 80 per cent of all church services in Wales were in Welsh.

↓

In the eighteenth century the Welsh Bible was used to teach the ordinary people of Wales, adults and children, to read. By 1761 just over half the population had learnt to read like this.

↓

More books were published in Welsh.

Religious leaders organized Sunday schools to educate ordinary people (there were no day schools for most children). The Welsh Bible was used in these Sunday schools to teach reading and writing well into the nineteenth century, and provided a basic education and a written standard of Welsh.

↓

Many Welsh people by the mid-nineteenth century could read in their mother tongue, Welsh.

Was the translation of the Bible into Welsh a turning point in Welsh history?

The importance of an event can be measured by asking the following questions:

- Was the event important to the people at the time?
- Were people's lives affected deeply by the event?
- How many people were affected?
- Were people's lives affected for a long time afterwards?
- Does studying the event help us to understand the world in which we live?

St Asaph memorial to Bishop William Morgan and the other translators of the Bible.

TASK

To help you understand these questions, a) discuss in pairs the significance of the long-term results of having the Bible in Welsh (pages 61–3), then b) copy out and complete these sentences.

The translation of the Bible was important to Elizabeth I's government because . . .

The translation of the Bible into Welsh was important to the ordinary people of Wales because it changed their way of life. When they went to church . . .

People's lives have been affected by the translation of the Bible into Welsh ever since the event because . . .

Learning about the translation of the Bible into Welsh helps to understand the world in which we live because . . .

I agree/disagree that the translation of the Bible into Welsh was a turning point because . . .

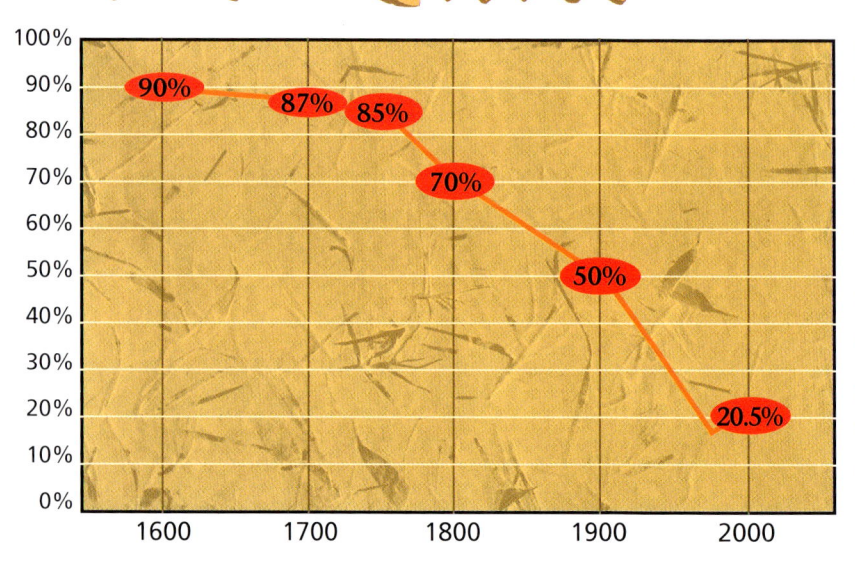

Percentage of the Welsh population speaking Welsh

Graph data points: 1600: 90%, 1700: 87%, ~1750: 85%, ~1800: 70%, ~1900: 50%, ~2000: 20.5%

These figures are approximate before 1891. The census of 1891 was the first to ask a question about the Welsh language.

Many of those recorded as Welsh-speaking in the 1891 census spoke only Welsh.

PART 2 1760–1914

2.1 How did Wales change between 1760 and 1914?

On the following pages 67–80 there are five sets of picture sources about life in Wales between 1760 and 1914. Each set of picture sources is followed by a set of written sources. They have been grouped together under five main headings:

People
Homes
Ideas and beliefs
Landscape
Work

Taken together these sources will begin to form a picture of life in Wales during this period.

These pictures are examples of **contemporary evidence**. This means that they come from the period. We can learn a lot about history just by looking at pictures.

Let us take this picture from page 73 as an example:

Think!
Looking at this picture for the first time you would need to ask more questions. What questions would you need to ask about the content of the picture?

Looking at picture sources

TASK 1

Make a list of things you can **definitely see** in this source.

These are the things which are visible, we can see them and can describe them from the source.

Once you have looked at the source, discuss what you have seen in more detail. Imagine that you are at the scene in the picture.

What can you hear?
What can you smell?
What can you touch?

By doing this you will be making deductions using the sources, very much like you did when you looked at Section 1.1 on life in Wales in the period 1485–1760.

Pictures are very useful as evidence to a historian. They are also important because they help us to ask more questions. You will find out more information about the events in this picture of Chartists at Newport when you read pages 134–5.

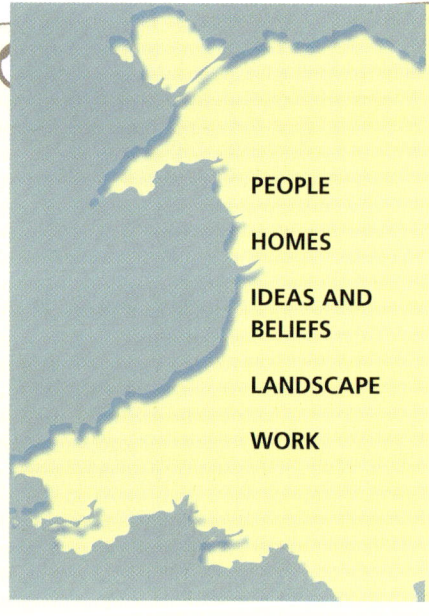

PEOPLE

HOMES

IDEAS AND BELIEFS

LANDSCAPE

WORK

Wales, 1760–1914, based on a selection of contemporary evidence

TASK 2

In small groups look closely at one set of picture sources – People **or** Homes **or** Ideas and beliefs **or** Landscape **or** Work.

1 Create a chart like the example on the left and write bullet points under your theme heading.

2 Write down what you can definitely see in the pictures.

3 One person from your group will report back to the rest of the class.

4 As the groups report their findings, fill in the other headings with information about what they have seen.

TASK 3

Below you will find a question about each of the themes.

People – Was life the same for everybody in this period?
Homes – What differences were there in people's homes during this period?
Ideas and beliefs – How did some people try to get their ideas heard during this period?
Landscape – How did the landscape of Wales change during this period?
Work – How did people's work change during this period?

In your groups and using the same set of pictures, try and work out more information about your theme to help you answer the question. Make suggestions, using the same technique you used in Task 1.

One person from your group will report back to the rest of the class. This should help everyone to build up a better picture of life in Wales during the period 1760–1914. Tell the class what your question was, and what you have found.

Each set of pictures gives evidence about changes in each of the themes. This was a period of great change across the whole of Wales. The whole period can be described as a turning point in Welsh history. Wales changed from being a mainly rural country with small towns and small-scale industry into a country where the majority of people worked in industries such as coal, steel, slate, tinplate and shipbuilding, and lived in industrial towns.

The information on your chart should help you to gain a general idea about life in Wales in the period 1760–1914. However, the picture is far from complete. There are many things about life in this period that the picture sources do not tell us.

We are now going to look at some **written** contemporary sources (sources written at the time). These sources will help us gain a fuller picture of life in this period.

TASK 4

Read through each set of contemporary written sources on pages 70–81, and pick out any new and interesting things that you did not see in the picture sources. Add these to your chart.

You now have a bigger picture of what life was like in the period and some of the changes that took place.

People

Looking at picture sources

1. Samuel Homfray, painted in about 1790.

2. Women washing clothes at Llanrwst Bridge, about 1799.

3. Robert Stephenson and the Committee for Britannia Bridge, 1853.

4. Tip girls leave work, south Wales, about 1879.

5. The John Cory Sailors' and Soldiers' Rest, Cardiff Docks, about 1903.

People

Looking at written sources

Key words

enclosure: the fencing-in and claiming of land by rich landowners
scythe: a hand tool for mowing long grass or crops

Source 1.
From William Cobbett, a traveller, in his book *Rural Rides* (1790):

In every village the decline can be seen. The farms get smaller and smaller and the farmworkers' houses are disappearing. Enclosure has meant a whole way of life vanishing overnight.

Source 2.
O. P. Jones, in his recollections of life in the 1890s:

I remember my father telling me of how things used to be once, how traditional farming life used to be. I even remember using the scythe, but as new machines like the mowing machine were brought in, the scythes were hung up on the barn wall.

Source 3.
Woman from Llwynypia, Rhondda, born in 1904:

We were more or less living with death every day. Every week there was someone being injured, someone being killed down the mines. There was always that tragedy hanging over us. I think it drew the families close together. That was my experience.

Source 4.
Man from Ogmore Vale, south Wales, born in 1906:

My father came from Somerset, and my mother came from Devon. Well, of course, the mines were developing, and the railways were developing, and of course there was no money working on the farms in the country, so that's what happened.

Homes

Looking at picture sources

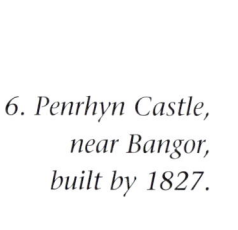

6. Penrhyn Castle, near Bangor, built by 1827.

7. A collier's home in the Rhondda Valley, 1875.

8. A cottage near Pontrhydfendigaid, Cardiganshire, in 1910.

9. Plasturton Gardens, Cardiff, in 1908.

Homes

Looking at written sources

Source 5.
Thomas Pennant, a traveller, in his book *A Tour of North Wales* (1777):

Bala has a vast trade in woollen stockings. During the winter females meet at one another's houses to knit, sit around a fire and listen to some old tale.

Source 6.
Walter Davies, a Welsh clergyman, writing in 1810:

A great deal of the counties of Anglesey, Caernarvon, Meirionydd and Montgomery are disgraced with cottages which are truly awful. One smoky hearth, for it could not be called a kitchen, and a damp litter-cell, for it cannot be called a bedroom, are frequently all the space given to a worker, his wife, and four or five children. The results are obvious; filth, disease and, frequently, early death.

Source 7.
H. J. Payne, south Wales health officer, in a report of 1849:

The overcrowding of houses has led to outbreaks of cholera which have killed hundreds. In one street in Cardiff there were 20 cases, and in 4 streets in Merthyr I counted 122 victims.

Source 8.
A former miner recalling his life around 1900:

I was in a lodging house with six or seven other miners. There was only three bedrooms so we would take turns to sleep in the beds. I would run home as fast as my legs would carry me to be the first to get a bath.

Source 9.
Manners at dinner, from a Holyhead magazine (1909):

*Do not sit a foot away from the table, nor right up against it.
Do not drink soup or broth from the end of the spoon. Do so from the side.
Do not make a noise when drinking, it is most unseemly.
Do not ask for a second helping of soup.
Do not bend heavily above the plate; remain as straight as possible, without being stiff.
Do not break bread with your teeth; do so with your hands.
Do not eat with the knife.
Never place the knife in your mouth.
Do not fill your fork as if you were loading a cart, with your knife; raise with the fork only what you can easily lift, and no more.*

Ideas and beliefs

Looking at picture sources

10. Protesters at Hirwaun, near Merthyr Tydfil, in 1831.

11. The attack of the Chartists on the Westgate Hotel, Newport, 4 November 1839.

12. Mass protest meeting at Merthyr Tydfil, 1875.

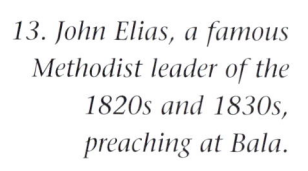

13. John Elias, a famous Methodist leader of the 1820s and 1830s, preaching at Bala.

Ideas and beliefs

Looking at written sources

Source 10.
William Lovett, a Chartist in the 1840s:

We are resolved to gain our rights peacefully if we can but by violence if need be. Those who would wage war on the millions should be aware!

Source 11.
A Merthyr newspaper report of 1848:

The town inns are full – little old men of 12/13 drinking beer and smoking their pipes with much importance. Hundreds go to the tavern for the want of something to do.

Source 12.
An extract from the report of a government inquiry in 1848 (writing about cottages at Llangynwyd in Glamorgan):

The cottages are expensively furnished. They contain, almost all of them, a handsome chest of drawers. On this usually rests a large and well-bound Bible. I saw everywhere coloured prints on the walls. They usually show scenes from the Bible or marriages – the marriage of Her Majesty and Prince Albert appears to be an especial favourite.

Source 13.
A School Commissioner, reporting in 1895:

Language difficulties have all but vanished in south Wales where parents have taught their children the value of English. The same effort must now be made in north Wales.

Source 14.
O. M. Edwards, later a school inspector, recalling his schooldays in the 1860s:

As soon as I spoke Welsh everyone laughed and a string was put around my neck with a heavy wooden token tied to it. I had put a similar device around the neck of a dog to stop it running after sheep.

Source 15.
Margaret Davies, writing about her life in 1900:

I could write a book on my early struggles with my seven children and a miner's home to contend with. The experience of three big strikes and many small ones hardened us. We were determined that more changes were needed to improve our lives.

Landscape

Looking at picture sources

14. Coal works near Neath, 1798.

15. The Britannia Tubular Bridge and the Menai Suspension Bridge, 1850.

16. Caernarfon in 1860.

17. Ferndale, Rhondda Valley, about 1900.

18. St Mary's Street, Cardiff, about 1913.

Landscape

Looking at written sources

Source 16.
Arthur Young, recalling his life in 1790:

I talked to a farmer who said he used to own many cattle but did not own as much as a goose by now. He said enclosures would be the ruin of Wales.

Source 17.
Benjamin Heath Malkin writing in 1803 about the Rhondda Valley:

The area was untamely wild. The people were thinly scattered, as well as miserably poor.

Source 18.
Edward Hadle, in his book *Wales in 1900*:

Newport and Cardiff have become huge exporting ports. The closeness of the south Wales coalfield has made the area the best and most economical in the world for heat producing. Millions of tons are exported annually.

Source 19.
A description of Llanelli from a Welsh newspaper in 1907:

The first thing that struck me was the filthy roads, the unhealthy smoke and a tram being pulled by a horse. There was no escaping the smoke because all the steel, tinplate and other works were planted in the centre of the place and houses built disorderly around them.

Work

Looking at picture sources

19. Shipping coal on the River Tawe, near Swansea in 1792.

20. Parys Mountain Copper Mine, about 1803.

21. Clasemont estate, Morriston, near Swansea, about 1820.

22. Miners in the Clog and Legging Level, Pontypool area, in about 1910.

23. Lipton's shop, Ammanford, about 1910.

Work

Looking at written sources

Source 20.
William Roberts, farm tenant, 1790:

When the winter months made life difficult, I used to keep warm with the clothes my wife made in our own house. She would make woollen clothes, and the money we made kept us going during the bad times.

Source 21.
Richard Howard, surgeon, 1840:

Most deaths are caused by a lack of food and long working hours which severely affect the health of the working classes.

Source 22.
A Welsh trapper, 1840:

I have been working as a trapper [opening and closing doors in the pits] since I was five years old. When I first went down the mine I couldn't keep awake, but I smoke a pipe now.

Source 23.
Maesteg miner, born 1886:

When you were using the mandrel [miner's pick] and tools, you'd get blisters on your hands. Whenever you wanted to urinate, you'd do it on your hands, and wash your hands in the urine. And that made them a lot better, and cured those blisters.

Source 24.
Pont-rhyd-y-fen woman, born 1910:

The girls went to work as maids. Or if they were a large family, the eldest daughter had to stay at home, to help the mother. The eldest daughter had no choice. And some would go out washing. Or sewing.

TASK 5

Six of all the written sources come from the period 1760–1810, six others from 1830–1850 and at least six others from the period 1880–1914.

1. Once you have decided which period they come from, prepare and complete a table like the one below to show which period the sources come from. If you have photocopies, you can cut them up and glue the sources under the correct headings.

1760–1810	1830–1850	1880–1914

2. Discuss in groups what the evidence tells you about each period. Make a list of five things you can definitely say about each period.

3. Write down answers to these questions under the title 'Change':
   a. What can you say changed during the period 1760–1850?
   b. What changes took place between 1850 and 1914?
   c. What were the biggest changes between 1760 and 1914?
      Try to make 5 bullet points.

Looking at statistics

Key word

census: a head count of all the people living in a country

There is a lot more information about life in the nineteenth century than for earlier periods in history. Governments carried out investigations about housing, working conditions and public health. In 1841 the first census was taken.

For the first time it was possible to know exactly how many people lived in Wales. Population figures before 1841 are based on estimates by historians. Look at the graph below of the population of Wales.

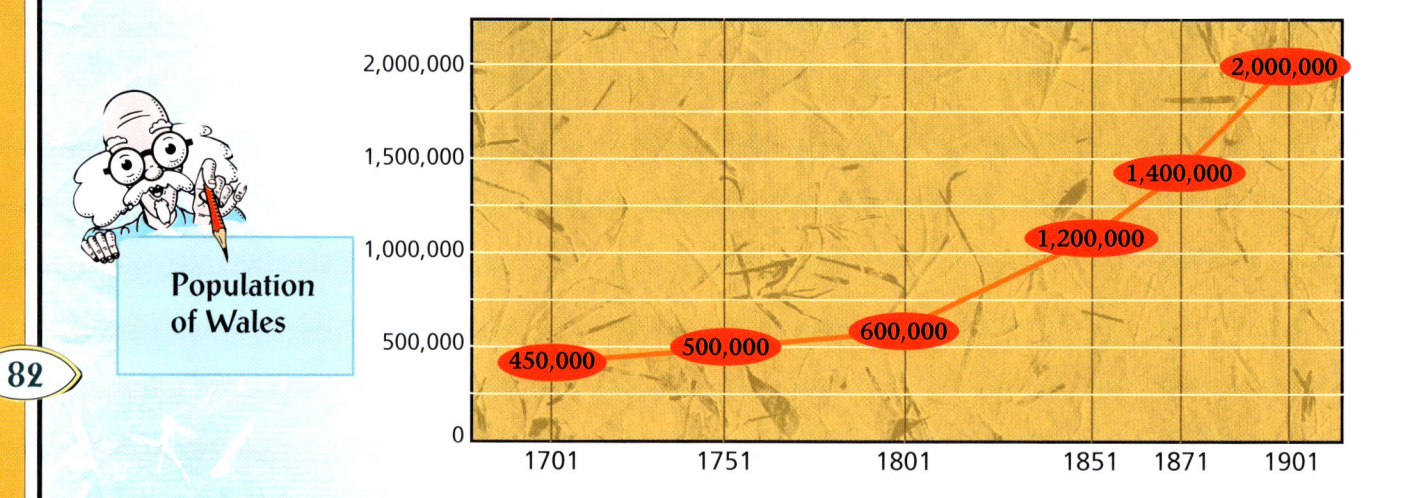

Population of Wales

Graph showing:
- 1701: 450,000
- 1751: 500,000
- 1801: 600,000
- 1851: 1,200,000
- 1871: 1,400,000
- 1901: 2,000,000

TASK 6

1. What is the overall picture the graph shows about growth in population between 1701 and 1901?
2. What happened to the population of Wales between 1801 and 1851?
3. Between which years on the graph was there the fastest growth in population?
4. Think of three questions that you could ask about the growth in population.
5. What information does the graph **not** give you?

The population figures give you a general idea about trends that were taking place in the nineteenth century. Some evidence, however, gives a lot more detail. For example, have a look at the table of figures about child death rates in Merthyr Tydfil between 1841 and 1853, and the bar chart for 1841 on the next page.

Child death rates in Merthyr Tydfil, 1841–1853

Year	Births	Deaths under 1	Deaths under 5	Total deaths
1841	1,482	247	554	974
1842	1,531	228	424	781
1843	1,574	226	403	810
1844	1,600	360	877	1,517
1845	1,694	309	590	1,082
1846	1,813	335	640	1,181
1847	1,759	385	788	1,434
1848	1,785	288	561	1,082
1849	1,791	428	998	2,925
1850	1,857	323	653	1,238
1851	2,056	374	761	1,481
1852	1,904	391	810	1,450
1853	2,006	400	772	1,483

Key word

mortality rate: the death rate in a particular area or period

Child death rates in Merthyr Tydfil, 1841

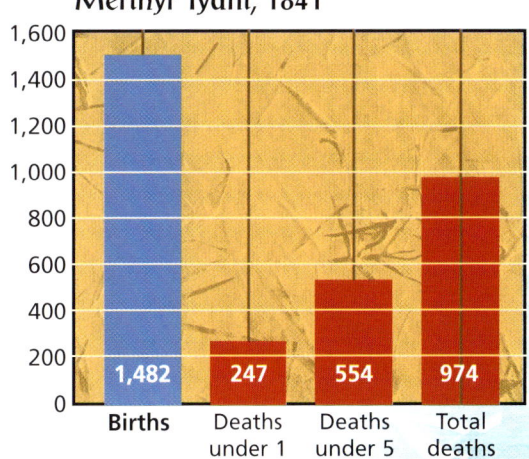

Bar chart showing: Births 1,482; Deaths under 1: 247; Deaths under 5: 554; Total deaths: 974.

TASK 7

1. Look at the bar chart for 1841. What does the chart tell you about the most dangerous age for a child born in Merthyr at this time?
2. About 50 per cent of those who died in Merthyr were children under five. Use the figures from 1841 to support this statement.
3. The figures tell us that children died at a young age in Merthyr. Suggest possible reasons for this.
4. Create a bar chart for the year 1849 similar to the one for 1841.
5. Why do you think the figures for 1849 stand out?
6. From the graph of population in Wales on page 82 we can see that the population of Wales continued to grow, despite the high mortality rate in places like Merthyr. Using the information shown in the table of child death rates in Merthyr, 1841–1853, can you say why this happened? Can you suggest any other reasons, not obvious from the table, why this may have happened?

These figures help to create a fuller picture of life in Merthyr between 1841 and 1853. They tell us that there was a high death rate in the town and that a large number of those who died were under five years old. The statistics do not tell us the reasons why. To find out we have to ask questions and then do some further investigation to create a fuller picture. For example, you will find more detail by reading written source 7 about homes.

Looking at maps

Historical information can also be presented as maps. The maps on these two pages help us to understand the changes which happened in Wales between 1760 and 1914, but they also show that different changes occurred in different parts of Wales. Not every part of Wales had the same experience in these years.

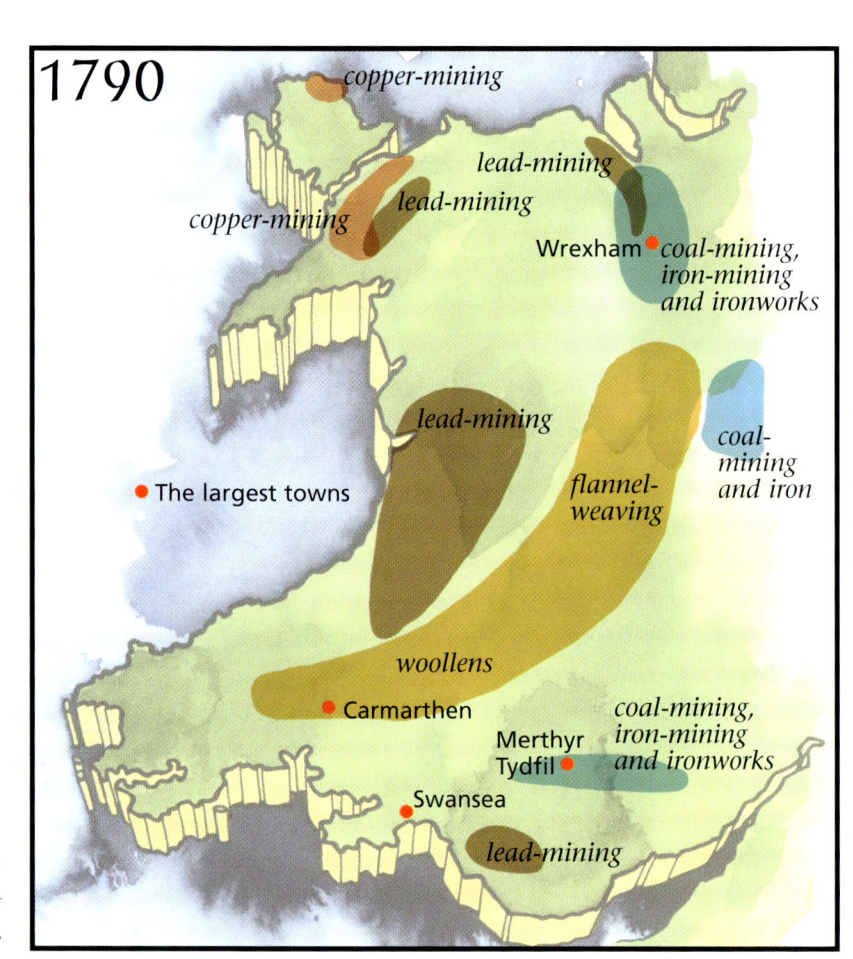

The main industries apart from agriculture

1790

- copper-mining
- lead-mining
- copper-mining
- lead-mining
- Wrexham — coal-mining, iron-mining and ironworks
- lead-mining
- flannel-weaving
- coal-mining and iron
- The largest towns
- woollens
- Carmarthen
- Merthyr Tydfil — coal-mining, iron-mining and ironworks
- Swansea
- lead-mining

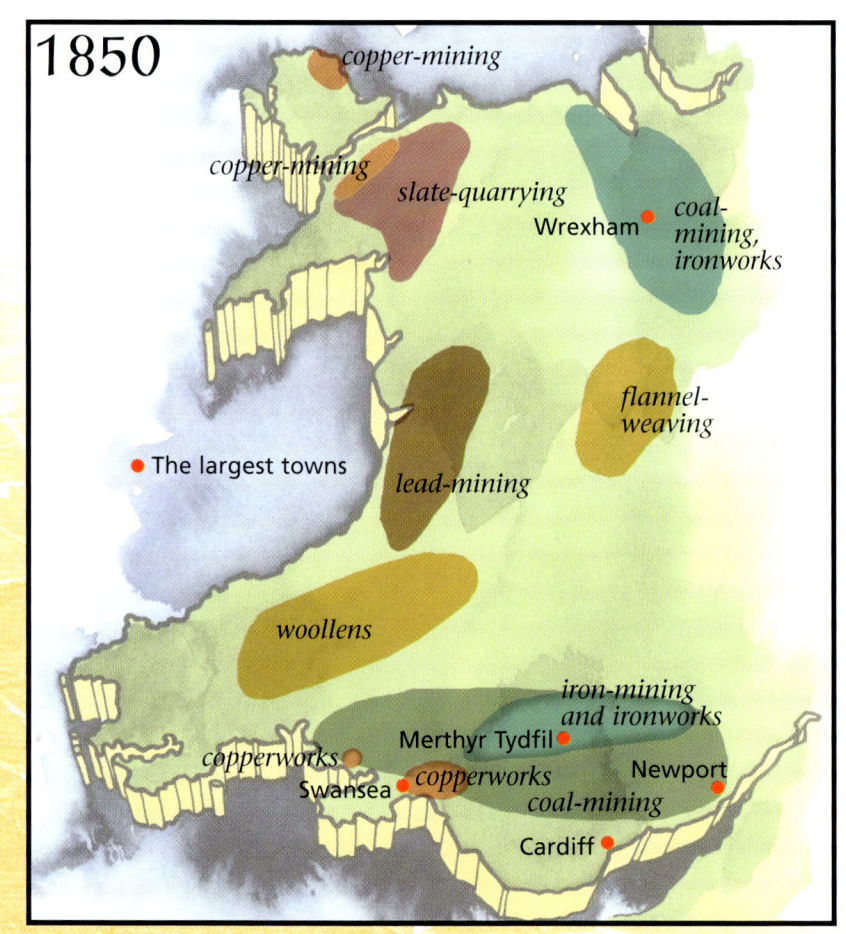

1850

- copper-mining
- copper-mining
- slate-quarrying
- Wrexham — coal-mining, ironworks
- flannel-weaving
- The largest towns
- lead-mining
- woollens
- copperworks
- Swansea
- Merthyr Tydfil — iron-mining and ironworks
- copperworks
- Newport
- coal-mining
- Cardiff

The main industries apart from agriculture

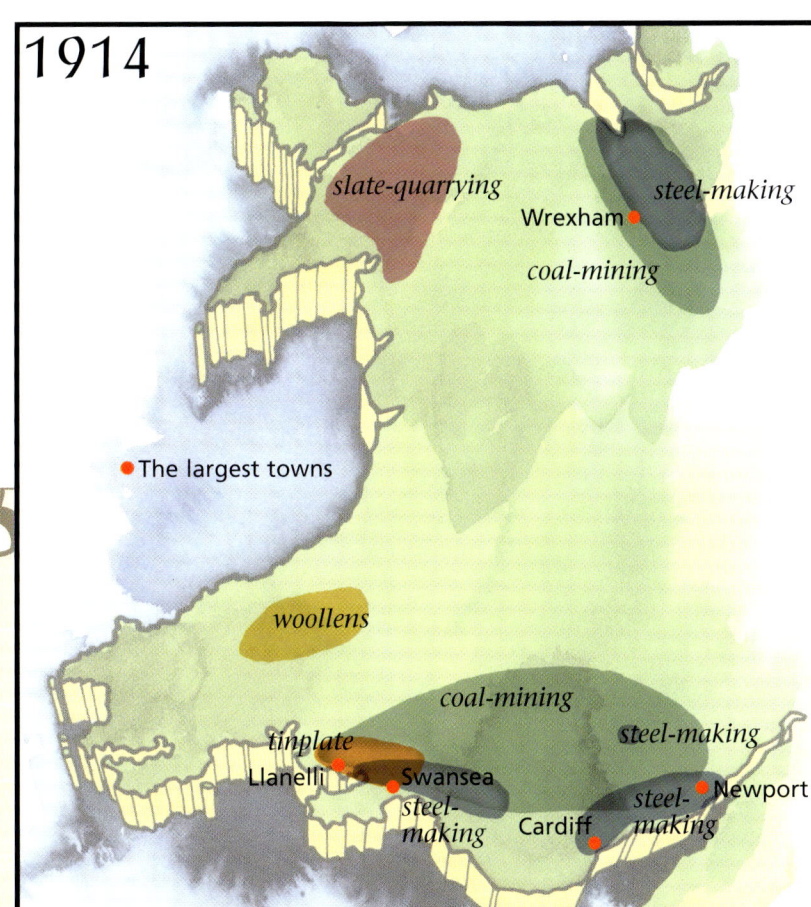

The main industries apart from agriculture

1914

- slate-quarrying
- steel-making
- Wrexham
- coal-mining
- The largest towns
- woollens
- coal-mining
- tinplate
- steel-making
- Llanelli
- Swansea
- steel-making
- Newport
- Cardiff
- steel-making

TASK 8

1. What were the main industries, apart from agriculture, in:
   a. north-west Wales in 1790, 1850 and 1914?
   b. north-east Wales in 1790, 1850 and 1914?
   c. mid-Wales in 1790, 1850 and 1914?
   d. south-west Wales in 1790, 1850 and 1914?
   e. south-east Wales in 1790, 1850 and 1914?

2. In which areas do you think most industry was concentrated by 1914?

3. Create a table to show how Wales in 1850 was different from Wales in 1790. Include the changes you can see in the maps and suggest how these changes may have affected the lives of the people. You can do this by using the following headings:
   - Work
   - Where people lived

4. Now do the same to compare Wales in 1914 with Wales in 1850.

5. Write a short paragraph summarizing how Wales had changed between 1790 and 1914.

You have now gained a general idea about life in Wales during the period 1760–1914. **You know that Wales changed from a country where the majority of people worked on the land into a country where the majority of people worked in the towns. In this period the towns and the population grew.** There were many advantages and disadvantages to this growth.

The following chapters will give us more detail about these changes.

2.2 Why was Wales on the move?

The Taff valley in about 1777.

Study these two pictures of the Merthyr Tydfil area in south Wales. Describe what you can see.

What changes do these pictures show in the landscape of this part of Wales?

Cyfarthfa Iron Works in Merthyr Tydfil, at the top of the Taff valley, in 1825.

The Jenkins family in 1800

William Jenkins

Megan

John

Daniel

Evan

On the farm

In this section we are going to look at the life of one imaginary Welsh family, the Jenkins family. This will help us to build a picture of life in Wales and how the events that occurred during this period changed the lives of the people of Wales.

A nineteenth-century photograph of a cottage in west Wales.

Wales in the eighteenth century was a land of large estates, owned by landlords, and small farms worked by families. Family labour meant that men, women and children did heavy manual work – looking after animals, hoeing, weeding, picking stones and gathering in the harvest.

William Jenkins and his family lived on a farm near Amlwch in Anglesey. William was a tenant farmer who paid rent to a local landowner. Some of his friends owned their own farms.

Key word

landlords: people who own land which is rented out to tenants

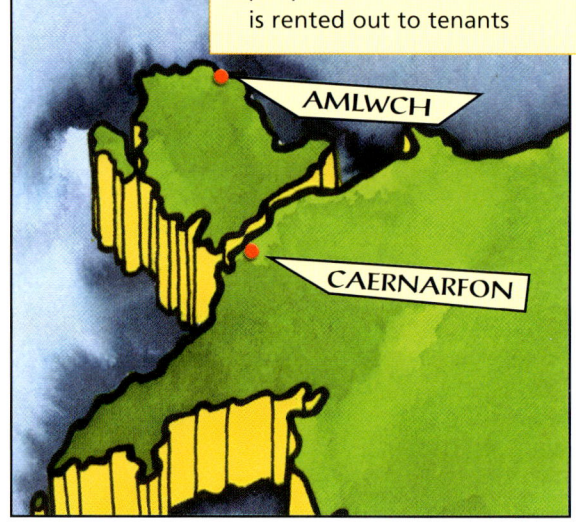

This painting by J. C. Ibbetson of the inside of a cottage in Glamorgan was painted in 1792.

Like most Welsh farms, the Jenkins farm was small, and had sheep, goats and cattle. The land was open and unfenced, and the animals would roam freely. The sheep would be sheared to produce wool. The family lived mostly on the food grown or raised on the farm. Their diet would be mainly bread, milk, butter, some vegetables and occasionally some bacon or other meat.

The only times the family would leave the farm were to go to market in Amlwch to sell butter or bacon, to help neighbours or to meet in bigger farms for song and celebration after harvest. Most Welsh towns were small and unimportant. Caernarfon was the main town in north-west Wales.

Think!
What do the two pictures tell you about life in Wales in the 1790s?

Corwen in north Wales was one such typical small town. Here is a drawing by Thomas Rowlandson from 1797.

Changes in farming

Key word

enclosure acts: laws forcing the fencing off of common land to form private property

New and improved methods of growing crops were becoming accepted in England by the end of the eighteenth century, but Welsh farmers with their smaller farms and poorer land were slow to use new methods and machines. The owners of large estates were the only ones who could afford to experiment or buy machines for farming. They could increase their profits and so wanted to increase the size of their farms.

Tenant farmers like William Jenkins were asked to pay higher rents and were forced out of their homes when they could not pay. Farmers who owned their own small farms came under pressure to sell.

If farmers refused to sell their land, landowners could appeal to Parliament. Parliament was run by the landowners. It passed laws, called enclosure acts, which banned farmers from grazing their animals on common land. This common land was very important because poor farmers relied on it to feed their animals. This virtually destroyed much of the Welsh farming community in north Wales. In Caernarfonshire, just 6 men owned 60 per cent of the land.

The changes in farming forced the sons of the Jenkins family to look around for other ways of making a living.

At the same time, new industries were starting in Anglesey as in other parts of Wales, and the promise of higher wages was very tempting to the Jenkins boys. By 1810 farming life in the Amlwch area, as in many other areas, had become difficult because of enclosures and because younger people were being lured into the new industries.

This photograph of farmworkers harvesting at Brechfa in west Wales was taken in about 1898, but farm work like this on the poorer farms had not changed much during the century.

In 1810 the Jenkins sons decided to leave their family farm. This would have been a very hard decision.

Think!
Look at the written sources 1, 6 and 16 in Section 2.1 (pages 70, 72, 77). In pairs, try to think of some reasons why the three Jenkins brothers decided to leave the farm and look further afield for work.

In **Ireland**, farmers faced similar difficulties. Life there became even harder because, unlike in Wales, there was no other employment there, and without work people faced starvation. Many moved away to live in America following a potato crop failure in Ireland in 1845, and many crossed the Irish Sea to Wales. Although some Welsh people emigrated, the growth of industries meant that there were jobs in parts of Wales.

TASK
We shall work in this unit to create a biography of the Jenkins family. This will be their history as seen through your eyes and it will help us to understand how change affected their lives. Using the template provided in the activity pack you will need to create pages that summarize what happened to them in this period.

Here you can start with page 1. Place a heading in the header box:

Life in farming at the start of the nineteenth century

Explain why the traditional way of life was under threat and how it affected the Jenkins family. Decide on a picture to place in the picture box.

Professor Info:
The changes in farming had forced many people all over Wales to look elsewhere for work. Work could be found in slate quarries, the copper industry, ironworks and coal mines.

Promise of Better Life

Why was Wales on the move?

- The population of Europe was increasing in the period 1750–1850. No one has been able to say exactly why this happened, but more children were born and over time people lived longer.
- By 1780 a steam engine was developed in England that could turn machinery. In England large factories full of these machines were built to make goods for the rising population.
- To build these machines, and to make these goods, iron was needed – Wales had plenty of iron ore and plenty of coal to feed the furnaces.
- In Wales, ironworks developed near coal mines, and these needed workers.
- Wales had workers, but they were not in the right places, so people moved from the farming areas to the industrial towns and villages.
- Farming changed because all these people needed to be fed.
- Roads, canals, railways and ports all developed in Wales because people and goods in Wales were 'ON THE MOVE'.

POPULATION OF WALES

Year	Population
1751	500,000
1801	600,000
1825	850,000
1851	1,200,000

POPULATION OF SOME TOWNS IN WALES

Where ?	1801	1851
Merthyr Tydfil	7,705	46,378
Swansea	6,099	21,533
Wrexham	4,039	6,660
Cardiff	1,870	18,351
Newport	1,135	19,323
Newtown	990	3,784
Ffestiniog	732	3,460

Cycle diagram:
- more people
- more goods needed
- more iron and coal needed
- more workers needed
- people moved from the country to the growing towns, especially near coal mines
- better transport needed to carry goods
- canals, railways, better roads and steamships built
- more food grown on bigger farms could be transported to the towns
- better farming techniques
- more food for sale to feed the population in the towns

The story of the Jenkins family

In 1810 the Jenkins sons left their farm in Amlwch. The three sons went off to work in different industries.

- John went to work in the slate quarries at Penrhyn, near Bangor.
- Daniel stayed on Anglesey and went to work in the Parys copper mines. 
- Evan moved further afield to the ironworks near Wrexham. 

In the next few pages you can find out what it was like working in each of these industries.

_____ Jenkins

Place and type of work:
_____

Why did the industry grow in this part of Wales?
_____

What was slate/copper/iron used for and how did this improve people's lives?
_____

What was it like to work in the industry?
_____

Was the move into the slate/copper/iron industry a positive or negative move for John/Daniel/Evan Jenkins?

TASK

To help gather the information as quickly as possible you need to divide into groups of three. One person should look at Option 1 (John Jenkins), one at Option 2 (Daniel Jenkins) and one at Option 3 (Evan Jenkins).

Read about the industry in which the family member worked, and look at the pictures. Once you have done so make a table like the one above right and write down the information required. The questions ask you to come to a judgement based on the available evidence. This is what historians do.

When you have completed your table you can share your findings with the other members of the group. Between the three group members you should then have information about the slate, copper and iron industries of Wales.

TASK

When you have information about all three sons, it is time to create the second page of our biography. The heading is '**The search for work**'. Describe briefly why all three brothers decided to move from the farm and what type of work was available for them. Where did they go? Why was industry growing in Wales? (Choose one example.)

Choose or draw an appropriate picture and place it with your second page.

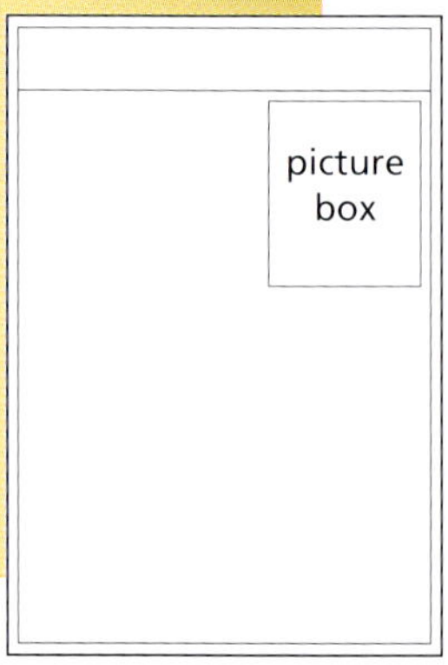

[picture box]

Option 1: John Jenkins on the move to the slate quarries

The slate industry of north Wales developed quickly. More houses were being built in the towns and they needed more roofs and floors. Later more schools meant more slates were needed for children to write on. John went to work at the slate quarry in Penrhyn, near Bangor.

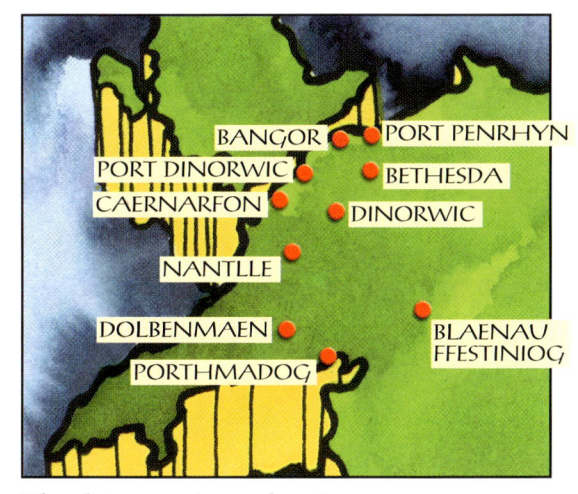

The slate quarries and ports of north-west Wales

Key word

tramroads: railtracks along which carts or wagons were pulled by horses

How did these slate quarries develop?

In 1765 Richard Pennant became owner of the Penrhyn estates, and he began to open up the world-famous Penrhyn quarries. Port Penrhyn harbour was also developed and houses were built for the increasing numbers of workers who worked in the Penrhyn quarries: 400 men in 1790, 2,000 men by 1850.

Other slate quarries soon opened at Dinorwic, Nantlle and Blaenau Ffestiniog and also grew fast.

All this led to transport developments. Richard Pennant, who became Lord Penrhyn, built roads and tramroads to transport the slates to Penrhyn Port, Bangor and Caernarfon. From there they would be shipped to Liverpool and then on to Europe and North America, or by canal to English towns.

North Wales became an important area of industry, exporting and importing as its ports grew.

By 1850, Welsh slate quarries produced over 90 per cent of the slate used in Britain.

The Penrhyn slate quarry painted by Henry Hawkins in 1832.

The slate quarries

Key word

silicosis: lung disease caused by breathing in silica dust

John and his team were paid for the amount of slate they quarried in a week. This was unfair because some areas of the quarry were harder to work than others.

John suffered from silicosis, because of the dust he was forced to breathe in after blasting the rock face.

Quarry workers worked long hours.

Disadvantages

Working in the quarries was difficult and dangerous. John had to climb ladders or hang on ropes to set explosives. In 1818 he fell off the ropes when setting explosives and was out of work for two months. There was no money for him during this time.

A drawing of Penrhyn slate quarry

Tourism in north Wales might well have developed without the slate industry.

The quarries ruined the local scenery and damaged the local environment.

Penrhyn Castle, the home of Lord Penrhyn, became a symbol that John hated. Lord Penrhyn made a lot of money on the back of John's suffering. By 1808 Lord Penrhyn was making a yearly profit of £7,000.

Penrhyn Castle.

Workers like John earned more money than when they were farming.

Housing was generally good and the availability of work also stopped John from having to move to other areas to work. It saved the communities of north Wales.

Farmers gained employment at a time when farming was in crisis:

Numbers working in slate in north Wales
1750   200
1800   6,000
1850   14,000

Advantages

Other transport in the area improved. The railway link between Holyhead and Chester opened in 1848, linking north Wales with the British rail system.

Ports also developed; there were services to Ireland, Liverpool and European and world ports.

The slate industry developed and improved transport in the region. Gwynedd became a vital economic link between Britain and Ireland.

The tourist industry boomed as a result of all these changes. By 1850 Llandudno had hotel rooms for 8,000 visitors.

The slate quay at Caernarfon in 1910.

Option 2: Daniel Jenkins on the move to the copper mines

Daniel, who was only thirteen, found work close to the family home in Amlwch. He worked in the copper mines of Parys Mountain, in Anglesey.

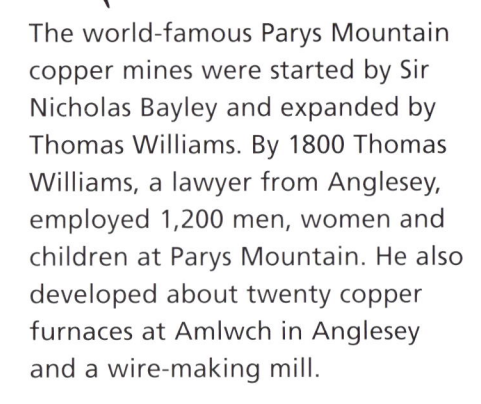

The world-famous Parys Mountain copper mines were started by Sir Nicholas Bayley and expanded by Thomas Williams. By 1800 Thomas Williams, a lawyer from Anglesey, employed 1,200 men, women and children at Parys Mountain. He also developed about twenty copper furnaces at Amlwch in Anglesey and a wire-making mill.

This is a picture of Parys Mountain copper mine painted by John Warwick Smith in 1792. Some historians believe that this is far too romantic a picture of the works and the landscape. Many local historians believe a better picture was the one below painted by William Havell in 1803/4. Which picture do you think gives a more realistic idea of what a copper mine was like? Why?

Working in the copper mine

You can decide whether on the whole Daniel was better off in the copper mines or not.

The copper mine and works were very unhealthy. Sulphur and sulphuric acid would pour from the mines into rivers. This affected Daniel's health.

The copper mine started out as a small hole but after furious blasting the middle fell in and Parys Mountain copper mine became a vast crater. The mines often became flooded in wet weather.

Disadvantages

Living in the area was not very pleasant. The water in the mine workings would be a strange green colour. Dust and fumes filled the air, and trees, plants and animals around the mine were scarce because of the poisoned air.

By 1802, the copper deposits at Parys Mountain were dwindling. Amlwch's importance then faded and there were riots there in 1817. When the industry in Amlwch died, Daniel, like many other workers, found himself on the move yet again.

As the Welsh iron and coal industries grew, copper began to lose its importance. Iron was easier and stronger to use than copper and could be produced more quickly.

Daniel would dangle on ropes to set charges to blow the sides. He would use gunpowder which was very dangerous.

When the copper ore reached the summit women (called 'copper ladies') and children were paid to break it into smaller pieces by hand and then to wash it. Daniel did this extremely hard work until he was 15.

Parys Mountain was important to the economy of Wales, Britain and Europe. Anglesey became the most important producer of copper in the world.

The copper mines were very important as they gave people like Daniel work at a time when farming was unprofitable. It saved many from starvation and gave them a sense of hope at desperate times.

Key word

smelting:
melting ore (rock containing metal) to get the metal out

The copper produced in Parys Mountain was processed in copper mills to make things for the rising population.

Advantages

Usage of copper during this period:
- pots and pans
- nails
- boilers
- tools
- ship building

Daniel was able to stay close to home. Many communities were kept alive. The mines were important for the local economy. Amlwch grew into a town of about 5,000 people by 1800. Jan Morris said in her book *The Matter of Wales*:

In its time Parys was the greatest enterprise in Wales. The nearby village of Amlwch, until then no more than a fishing hamlet, was transformed into a tough and lively industrial town.

Hafod copper works in Swansea, painted by Henry Gastineau in about 1830.

Copper ore was shipped from Parys Mountain to Swansea in south Wales, where there was plenty of cheap coal to use in the smelting mills. By 1820, 90 per cent of Britain's copper was produced in Swansea, so this helped the economy of south Wales too.

Option 3:
Evan Jenkins on the move to the ironworks

Evan looked east towards Wrexham and Flint for a job in industry. There had been small-scale ironworks in Wales for quite some time, as this painting by Paul Sandby of an iron forge between Dolgellau and Barmouth in 1776 shows.

Evan had heard of new ironworks in north-east Wales. There a businessman called John Wilkinson turned the furnaces at Bersham and Brymbo into key European industries. In 1801 a 19-tonne iron plate was transported from his furnaces on a specially constructed cart, pulled by eight horses. This was the largest weight ever carried by land in Britain.

Evan moved in 1810 to work at the Brymbo ironworks. He never saw his brothers again.

The main ironworks in north-east Wales

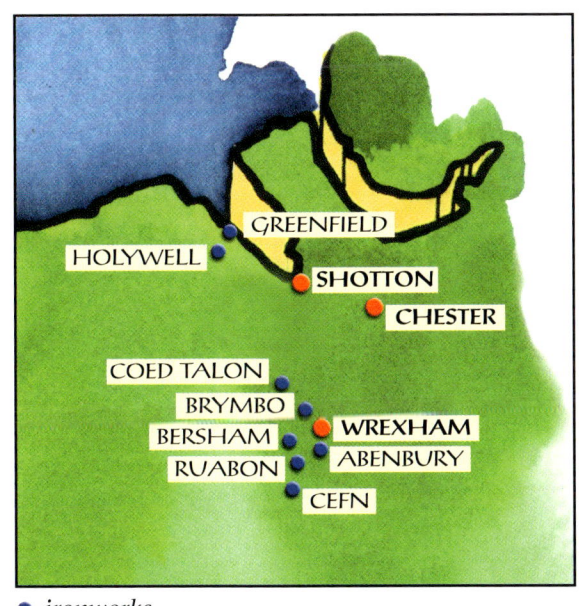

- ironworks

> To make iron, iron ore and limestone were loaded into the charcoal furnace, though charcoal was soon replaced at Wrexham and Merthyr by coke from the nearby coal mines. The red-hot liquid iron was then drawn from the furnace, leaving the slag.
>
> The liquid ore was poured into 'pigs' or moulds, but 'pig-iron' was not very strong. 'Puddling' was later invented to strengthen the finished iron. The slag was dumped on nearby hillsides in slag heaps.

J. C. Ibbetson painted this scene of an iron forge in Merthyr Tydfil in 1789. The men are removing iron from the furnace and then hammering it into shape.

The iron industries of north-east Wales had been doing pretty well, especially during the Napoleonic Wars (1793–1815). It was said that both the French and British used cannon-balls and shot made in north Wales. The widespread use of the steam engine in factories led to further growth in the industry.

The work close to the furnaces was difficult and dangerous but the pay was better than Evan could have expected from farming.

The iron industry grew in south Wales too. In the 1780s a new method of producing iron known as 'puddling' was discovered at the Dowlais ironworks near Merthyr Tydfil. This method produced better-quality iron that could be used to make small as well as large iron parts. In south Wales there was plenty of coal, and ironworks could be built in the coalfields where many small coal mines developed.

Dowlais ironworks, painted by George Childs in 1840

The rise in the price of goods after 1815 meant that it was very difficult to live on the wages that some ironworkers were given.

The demand for iron led to working practices such as employing young children.

There were many injuries and accidents, many of them involving children.

The furnaces were very hot and the working hours were long.

Disadvantages

Workers' housing was very poor. Evan had to share his house with many other workers. Profit became more important than people in the industrial areas.

Many ironworkers had to buy goods at the owners' shops. These were called 'Tommy shops' or truck shops, and the prices were higher than in other shops. This forced many workers into debt.

Advantages

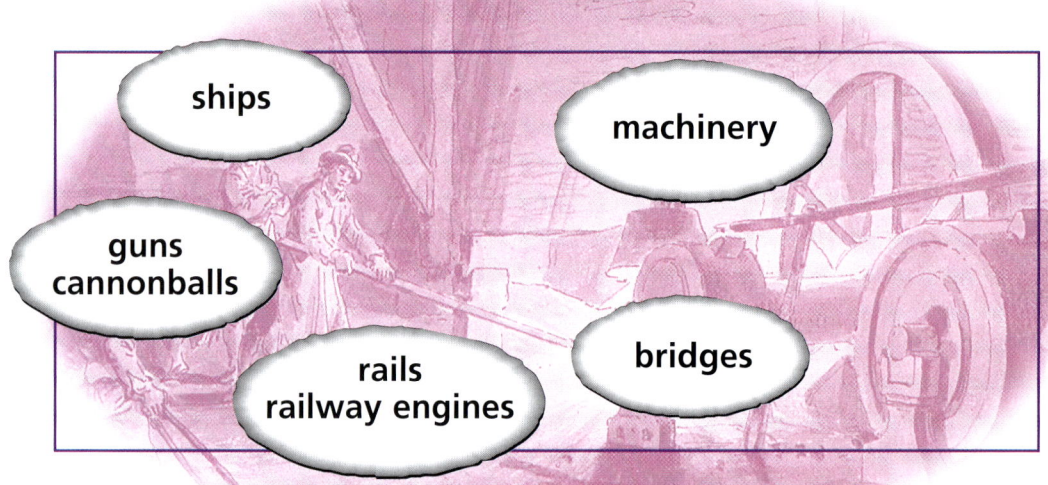

Many new things could now be made that would have been impossible to make without iron, such as complicated factory machinery and steam engines.

One reason why Britain won the Napoleonic Wars with France by 1815 was that John Wilkinson's furnaces were producing cannonballs at a very fast rate.

Tools and machinery made of iron could be produced faster and more cheaply in ironworks and factories than previous wooden, copper and hand-made items.

Usage of iron during this period:
- ships
- machinery
- guns cannonballs
- rails railway engines
- bridges

By 1800 nearly 50 per cent of the iron produced in Britain came from south Wales. This led to thousands of workers moving there.

The success of the iron industry in north-east Wales persuaded other businessmen to move to the area and invest money in the ports and improved transport.

The iron workers in north-east Wales were among the best-paid manual workers during the first half of the nineteenth century.

The growth of the iron industry provided Evan Jenkins and other Welshmen with much needed work.

The long walk south

How would you travel to south-east Wales from north-west Wales today? What options are there?

- motor car
- bus
- railway
- walk

Even today the journey can be difficult. There is no motorway through the middle of Wales, and there is no direct railway line.

Whichever way you go, the journey is a long one even by modern standards, and in 1817 there was, of course, no motor car, bus or railway.

A typical rail journey today from Swansea to Bangor:

Swansea	0717
Cardiff (change)	0844
Newport	0859
Crewe (change)	1117
Bangor	1249

Think!
How long is a typical journey by train from Swansea to Bangor? Can you work out the route by looking at a map?
(By comparison, the train journey time from Swansea to London is just over 3 hours on average.)

Why did Daniel Jenkins move south?

As a young boy he had worked on his father's farm. The younger members of the family had been forced to leave the farm because they could not make a living. Daniel had moved to the copper works, but in 1817 the copper mine closed and he lost his job. After a fruitless search for work he decided to move to Merthyr in south Wales where he had heard that there was work. Daniel left Amlwch and Parys Mountain in 1817 to head for south Wales. Staying in Amlwch was not an option, and many like Daniel had to look further afield for work. He was poor. There was only one real travel option open to him – he would have to walk.

Travelling on the roads was not that straightforward, as we shall see. Look back at the pictures of the landscape. What difficulties did it pose for the traveller?

Travelling was difficult

In 1764 the Methodist preacher John Wesley rode around parts of Wales. These are two extracts from his diary:

Between Llanidloes and Tregaron, 25 July
Having wandered for an hour on the mountains, through rocks and bogs and cliffs, we with great difficulty got back to the little house near the bridge.

Tuesday 31 July
We set out for Glamorgan and rode up and down steep and stony mountains for about five hours to Laugharne. We went up to the Llanstephan ferry where we were in some danger of being swallowed up in the mud before we could reach the water.

Think!
Daniel travelled from north to south Wales to look for work. He was heading for Merthyr, over 200 miles away. His journey would take him up mountains, along valleys, across desolate moorland and across rivers. The weather could be wet. How long do you estimate that the journey might take?

Roads

Key word

turnpike trusts: private companies formed to build and repair roads and to collect tolls to pay for the roads.

Arthur Young travelled in Wales in 1776. He described the road from Chepstow to Newport as being little more than a rocky lane. There were huge stones the size of horses and massive holes.

In 1817 when Daniel left Anglesey he would have crossed the Menai Straits by ferry. When he got to the other side he would have become aware of changes being made to improve the roads. In 1811 the road engineer Thomas Telford had been appointed to repair the road between London and Holyhead. By 1817 work was in progress, although it was not complete until 1827, a year after the Menai Bridge was built.

Telford described how difficult it was to build the road from Shrewsbury to Holyhead.

This road established through a rugged and mountainous district, partly along the slope of rocky cliffs, and across inlets of sea, where mail and other coaches can now travel at the rate of ten miles per hour, was indeed a very difficult job which took fifteen years of continuous hard work.

New roads and turnpike trusts

Groups of business men got together to improve roads so that they could get their products to ports and towns more quickly. They formed turnpike trusts to build and maintain roads, but to cover their costs and make a profit they charged people tolls for using the roads. This angered many people in Wales who now had to pay to travel or move their animals from their farms to market.

As Daniel made his journey south he would have seen these toll-gates.

Canals

> **Key word**
>
> **navvies:** labourers who worked on the canals

On his journey Daniel may have passed through the towns of Newtown and Welshpool where woollen cloth was by then produced by machines in factories. Here he would have seen the last section of the Montgomery Canal being built. The canal linked Newtown with Welshpool, north-east Wales, and the large English cities of Birmingham and Manchester.

When he arrived in Merthyr he would have seen the end of the Glamorgan Canal which linked Merthyr to Cardiff via the Taff valley.

Canal building in Wales began in 1790 with the building of the Glamorgan Canal down the Taff valley. It was opened in 1794 and, like most canals being built at that time, it was used to ferry coal and iron from the industrial areas to the ports. Digging the canals in such steep-sided valleys was difficult and many hundreds of navvies were used to do the hard digging. Heavy goods could then be transported much more easily in canal barges than on the backs of mules or in horse-drawn carts.

Another important town for woollen production was Llanidloes. This photograph of a Llanidloes woollen factory was taken in about 1880.

A canal lock at Pontypridd on the Glamorgan Canal in the 1930s.

Railways

Richard Trevithick's moving steam engine.

On his journey south Daniel may have heard stories about a new form of transport, especially as he was going to Merthyr. It was here in 1804 that an engineer called Richard Trevithick made a name for himself. He was the the first man to develop a moving steam engine to run on rails. He did it as a bet. On 12 February 1804, Trevithick's machine pulled a wagon containing 10 tonnes of iron and 70 men, from the Penydarren Ironworks in Merthyr Tydfil as far as Abercynon. He won his bet, but his idea was not taken up and he was to die in poverty.

It was another twenty-five years before railway building began to take off. In 1829 George Stephenson demonstrated his famous locomotive train, the Rocket. The first railway line in Wales was built in 1841 between Merthyr Tydfil and Cardiff. Other lines soon followed where they were used to transport goods from the growing industries to port towns like Caernarfon and Bangor in the north, Ellesmere Port and Liverpool in the north-east, Fishguard, Cardiff, Swansea and Newport in the south.

Think!
Think of ways in which railways affected people's lives.

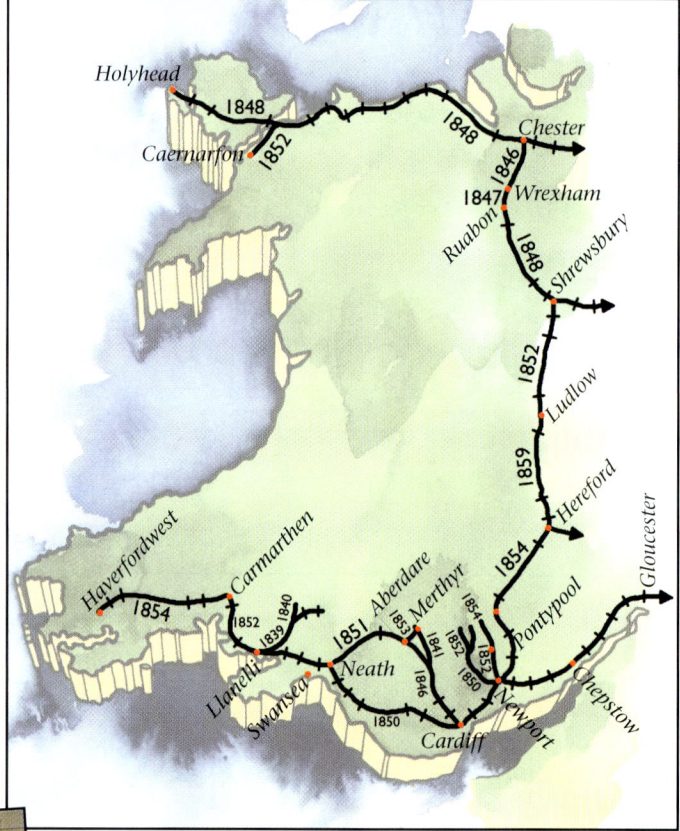

The railways of Wales built by 1854 (with dates of completion)

Many people were afraid of the new railways and thought that they were too dangerous to be used to carry people. Nevertheless, passenger trains soon began to be an important means of travel.

Daniel would not have seen many of these developments which were to make travelling much easier from the middle of the nineteenth century. His journey would have taken weeks, or perhaps even months, travelling on foot. He would have needed money for food for a long journey, so he might have stopped often on the way to work on a farm.

Here is an extract from a diary of a real person, Evan Rees, who moved with his family from Pembrokeshire to Aberdare in 1850:

The family had to walk the whole way. They placed all the furniture they considered important on the back of a cart and started to walk behind it, on a journey that would take them four days and three nights.

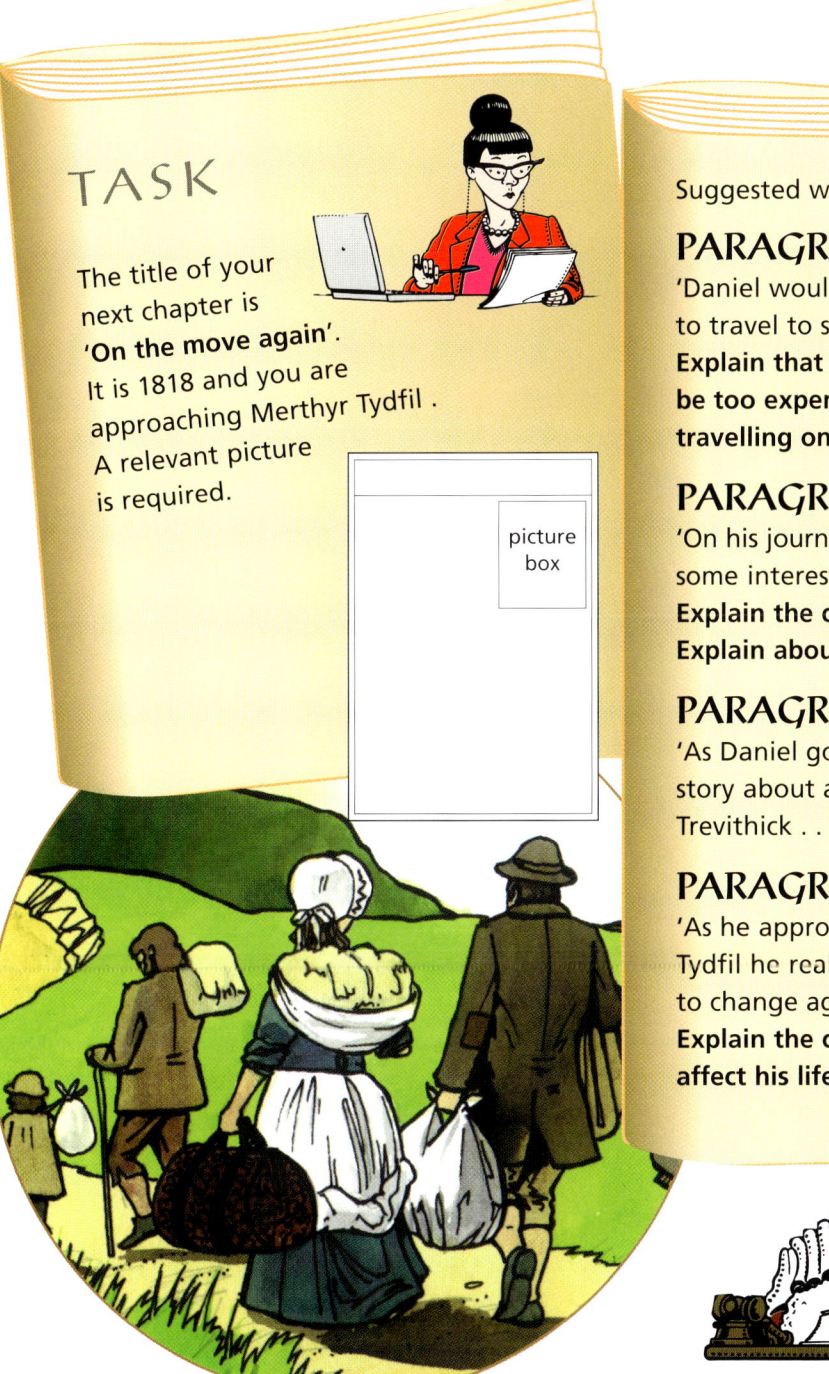

TASK

The title of your next chapter is **'On the move again'**. It is 1818 and you are approaching Merthyr Tydfil. A relevant picture is required.

picture box

Suggested writing frame:

PARAGRAPH 1:
'Daniel would have taken a long time to travel to south Wales . . .'
Explain that some forms of transport would be too expensive. Explain the difficulties of travelling on the roads.

PARAGRAPH 2:
'On his journey south Daniel would have seen some interesting changes in transport . . .'
Explain the changes being made to roads. Explain about the building of canals.

PARAGRAPH 3:
'As Daniel got near to Merthyr he heard a story about a Cornishman named Richard Trevithick . . .'

PARAGRAPH 4:
'As he approached the lights of Merthyr Tydfil he realized that his life was going to change again . . .'
Explain the changes that were likely to affect his life.

A new beginning!

Daniel arrived in Merthyr Tydfil in 1818 after hearing that there was plenty of work there for men who could make iron or dig for coal.

Daniel was able to get a job in the ironworks there, although the coal mines were also crying out for workers.

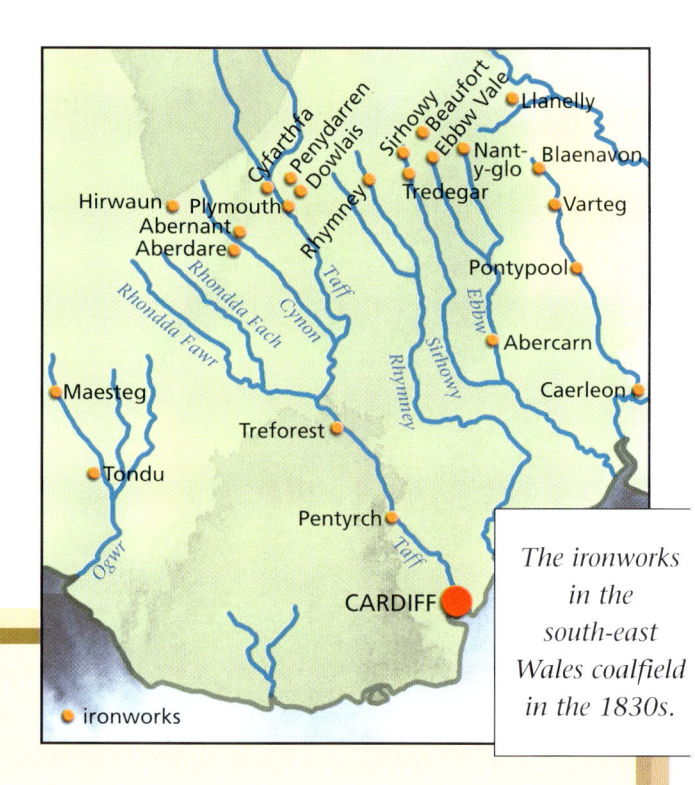

The ironworks in the south-east Wales coalfield in the 1830s.

The iron and coal industries in south Wales

South Wales industry developed quickly due to the fact that ironworks could be built very close to the coal mines. As coal in large quantities was necessary for producing iron, transport costs could be kept to a minimum.

The Dowlais ironworks in Merthyr Tydfil was a growing business, managed by John Guest. Soon other operators moved in. Richard Crawshay of Yorkshire opened the ironworks in Cyfarthfa, and his son William took over management of these works. The success of the four world-famous ironworks of Merthyr Tydfil – Dowlais, Cyfarthfa, Plymouth and Penydarren – led to a huge growth in the town.

The ports of Swansea, Cardiff and Newport also became very important, linking the iron and coal industries with the rest of the world.

The towns grew and grew as more workers arrived to find work.

This is a picture of the Bute furnaces at Rhymney, painted by John Petherick in about 1830. What do you think the painter thought about the iron industry from looking at this picture?

These ironworks became enormous in size and people flocked to south Wales from within Britain and from other countries to find work there.

Early coal mines

The massive growth in the iron industry led to a huge rise in the demand for coal which was needed to make iron. The development of trains, which needed coal, also added to the growth in demand, and led to the transportation of coal from the collieries to the ports from where it could be shipped all over the world, for use in steam trains and steam ships.

An early coal mine in 1792, painted by J. C. Ibbetson.

Many women did heavy manual work in early coal mines.

Most large-scale coal mines did not open in south Wales until the 1850s, but the success of the coal industry was guaranteed because of the large number of iron furnaces in the area.

Think!
From the pictures on this page, what do you think were the main difficulties and dangers of working in coal mines in the early nineteenth century?

The bottom of a shaft in a coal mine: a collier is being lowered from above and the baskets of coal are waiting to be hoisted to the surface. The light came from candles; here you can see one in the boy's hands and another fixed in the roof.

The development of south Wales was dramatic and had a positive as well as a negative effect on the lives of people in Wales, Britain and the world. People like Daniel also became acutely aware of the differences between those who owned the collieries and iron furnaces and those who worked in them. This feeling of class difference began to affect life in Wales more and more during this period. This painting of the Cyfarthfa Hunt in 1830 shows the owners of industry in the Merthyr area meeting socially.

A Tredegar colliery worker in about 1860.

TASK

1. What can you suggest about the owners of industry from the picture?

2. What can you suggest about the Welsh miner from the picture?

3. How do the pictures of worker and owners differ?

4. What questions would you like to ask about the pictures and the people shown in them?

Hannah goes into service

When Daniel moved to Merthyr he met a girl named Hannah. She had moved to Merthyr from a village called Llangadog in west Wales in the hope of finding work. She had been lucky enough to get work as a domestic servant to the family of William Crawshay, the ironworks owner. Daniel and Hannah wanted to get married but they had to save up enough money between them to be able to rent a house, and this took some time. In 1825 the Crawshay family and servants moved into the newly built Cyfarthfa Castle.

Hannah's life as a domestic servant was very different from that of the women of the Crawshay family.

Hannah slept in the servants' quarters at Cyfarthfa, which were usually bare attic rooms shared with two or three other servant girls. Hannah, as a scullery maid, had to get up at 5 o' clock in the morning to light the kitchen fires, and then work all day doing the hard labour in the kitchens, like carrying coal, cleaning vegetables, washing pots and pans. Her tasks would not be over until late at night when all the dishes from the Crawshays' dinner had been washed and dried. Still, at least she was sure of getting some good food.

Even among domestic servants, people had different jobs. This picture shows the outdoor staff at Cyfarthfa in the 1880s. There would be grooms, gamekeepers, stable-boys and gardeners. Can you guess from this picture what these servants did?

Cyfarthfa Castle was a splendid palatial castle, with 72 rooms and 15 towers, with heating and warm fires in all family rooms but only some of the servants' quarters. Food was served in a large dining hall and the Crawshay family would always dress for dinner.

Mrs Rose Crawshay did not work for money, of course, but would supervise the servants to make sure that the household was run efficiently. She spent much time visiting other wealthy families or receiving guests.

Women were not allowed to vote (women were not allowed to vote until 1918, and even then it was only wealthier women who could vote), and it was thought improper for them to take part in political discussions or decisions. They were dependent on their husbands for money – even the wealthy women – and had very few rights in law.

Many wealthy women felt that it was their duty to help poor people around them in some way and so did charitable work. Mrs Crawshay was particularly active. She organized soup kitchens in several local villages for poor people to receive soup three times a week, and this arrangement lasted for 30 years. She also opened seven free libraries to encourage people to read. She believed that women should be educated and should have some political rights. She was one of the first people to be elected to the local School Board, the committee elected to run schools in the county.

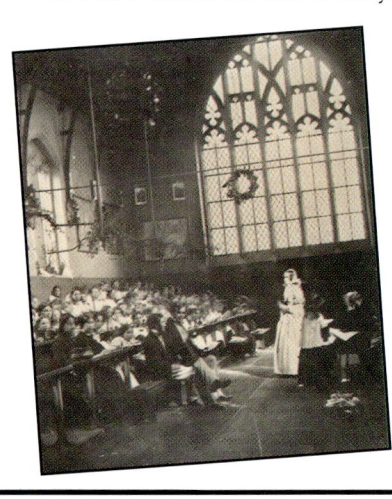

A ball given in the huge wagon shed at Cyfarthfa for the wedding of Rose to Robert, William Crawshay's son, in 1846.

Mrs Crawshay and her daughters.

Lady Charlotte Guest giving an address at a prize day in Dowlais School

Professor Info:

One of Rose Crawshay's friends was Lady Charlotte Guest at Dowlais. Lady Charlotte was a scholar who translated medieval Welsh tales into English under the title *The Mabinogion.* She also set up schools in Dowlais for children of the workers. She later unofficially ran the Dowlais ironworks during periods when her husband was ill.

When Daniel and Hannah got married, Hannah had to leave the Crawshays' service in order to live in a rented house with Daniel and raise children. Most people felt that once married, women should not go out to work, especially if they had children. Housing was so scarce that even with their few savings they could not afford to rent more than a small house shared with another family of four.

For most women in employment the work was hard, the hours were long and living conditions poor. As we have seen, women worked in coal mines and ironworks at this time, and so did many children. Sometimes whole families worked together since the women could not afford to stay at home. Women were paid less than men for doing similar heavy manual work, and children were paid very poorly.

It was not all doom and gloom, however. Single women now had their own money, so they did not have to rely on men as much as in the past. In north Wales especially, women became the main owners of shops and public houses.

Women hauliers in the Rhondda, in about 1880.

Think!
- Why do you think that parents allowed their children to work?
- What were the advantages and disadvantages for Hannah in getting married?
- How has the position of women in the twenty-first century changed from this period?

TASK

Add one page to your biography of the Jenkins family. The heading is **'In service to the Crawshays'**. Describe Hannah's work as a servant and the different life that Mrs Crawshay had. Choose a picture.

Was life good or bad for Daniel and Hannah? Looking at the evidence

Source A
The courts are often awash with mud, filth and wasted food, and it is here that the Irish and Welsh make their beds. All the filth from the houses is thrown on top of these. It is impossible to walk the streets in wet weather, horses and carts sink knee deep in the foul mixture.

Newspaper, 1850

Source B

Source D
The people use chamber pots and freely dispose of the contents into the streets in front of their houses, or into the rivers. Men relieve themselves wherever they please and children are placed out in chairs to do their necessary business.

Government inspector, 1849

Terraced housing built in Merthyr Tydfil in about 1845. In this terrace there were upper houses with two rooms each, and basement houses had one room each.

Source C
I have inspected a region called Bethesda Gardens near Pontshorehouse. It is truly awful. The families often lived in cellars, which were under the roads, and filth would flow into them from streets and buildings. In one house the gutters flowed freely inside them.

Health report, 1853

Source E
Sands American Circus performed at the Cyfarthfa Castle Field at 2.30 p.m. to around 1,300 people and again at 7.30 to around 2,500–3,000 people.

Newspaper article, 1844

Source F
There was only one pure water fountain for the whole of Merthyr Tydfil. It is not uncommon to see a 100 people waiting their turn. Women have told me that they sometimes wait 6, 8 maybe 10 hours for their turn. Some have been awake all night queuing.

Health inspector, 1830

Source H
The vibrant life of the Rhondda was an ideal place for balladers like Dic Dywyll to make their name. They would frequent the markets and taverns, selling their poetry and song. It was little wonder that the 1820s saw a resurgence in the Eisteddfods of Wales.

Hefin Jones, who wrote a book about Dic Dywyll

Source G
The people have a tendency to fetch their water from a hole situated near the cemetery of capel Bethesda. This water has come to the hole by being drained through the cemetery itself. One can only imagine its taste and foulness.

A cholera inspector, 1835

Source I
There were many taverns in Merthyr and the surrounding towns and cities. There were certainly enough bad things to say about them, but they were also a hive of activity and the central part of many community lives.

Magazine article, 1970

Source J

Early Friday morning a large rat attacked Mr James Evans's son. The boy was in his mother's arms when the boy's movements awaked her. She awoke to find the bedclothes awash with blood and found the rat eating her son's side.

Newspaper article, 1839

Source K

The children have been amused by an exhibition of wax works in the western portion of the market-house.

Newspaper, 1842

Source L

The diversity of people to behold in the area is unlike any other. The Welsh mix with the Irish and the Scottish and the English and mingled here and there are strange foreign accents belonging to those who come to seek a better life. The cosmopolitan nature of life here certainly draws those looking for adventure and high spirit.

The Times newspaper, 1856

Source M

There remains little doubt that death rates were high because health issues were ignored by the owners of industry as well as by the people themselves. Both are to be blamed for not wanting to spend money on hygiene. It is little wonder this age deserves the title 'the Slaughter of the Innocents'.

Academic historian Alison Baggott, History of Wales (2001)

Source N

Local sporting contests grew very popular and prize-fighting, cock-baiting and dog-fighting became a way of life.

Sporting Digest magazine describing Cardiff in 1840

Outside the Lord Raglan pub in Merthyr Tydfil in the 1870s.

TASK

1. Using the evidence in Sources A–N, make a list of the good things about Daniel and Hannah's life in Merthyr Tydfil, and then a list of the bad things.

2. You are now in a position to complete another page in your story of the Jenkins family. The title of this section is **'A better life?'**. By the end you must decide (give an interpretation) whether their lives were changed for the better or for the worse.

Again, remember that your picture should show an interpretation about their lives in Merthyr Tydfil.

picture box

Why did children die so young?

Many children died at a young age in Wales at this time, especially in the south Wales mining regions.

Key words

life expectancy: the number of years a person is likely to live

trapper: a child whose job was to open the trap-doors down a coal mine for trams carrying coal

My son Edwin was a lively and mischievous little boy but three years in the pits have changed him. He's weak and he can hardly walk. I send him to the pits every day, I have a big family and they need feeding.
Gilbert Sharpe from Merthyr Tydfil, 1840s

Life expectancy in 1848

Tregaron, west Wales: 41 years 9 months

Merthyr Tydfil: 18 years and 2 months

I have been working in the pits since I was 5 years old. When I first went down I could not stay awake, but now I smoke a pipe.
The words of an unnamed trapper from Wales in 1842

In areas I studied in Wales between 1841 and 1847, 11,454 children were born and 4,278 children died before reaching their fifth birthday – 37.3%. These drastic figures speak volumes about the terrible conditions.
William Kay, Health Inspector, 1854

Although deaths as a direct result of starvation are rare, there is no doubt that many of the deaths occur amongst the working classes because of a lack of food, long working hours, lack of clothing, and the wet damp conditions in which they live and work.
Health Inspector, 1849

They were killed by their parents!

Not literally killed, but killed through ignorance. Parents would often bring home deadly diseases and infections from work which would kill a small child in a matter of days. Also babies would eat and drink the same as their parents. If their parents lived on potatoes alone, rotten vegetables or contaminated water, the danger signs were there. Today we know a lot more about health issues and how diseases are passed on.

They were not strong enough

A lack of proper food meant that children lacked the strength to fight diseases and infections. Typhoid, cholera and tuberculosis killed in their hundreds and thousands. A lack of sewerage systems and poor sanitary conditions were the main causes, and ignorance led to a lack of will to do anything about it.

The work in the mines

Children would often work in very dangerous conditions. The opening and closing of doors in the mines was always done by children. The damp, dirty, unhygienic conditions, combined with the fact that they would work in total darkness, would reduce their life expectancy. The trappers, as they were called, were coffin fodder!

Children's work in industry

Large numbers of children were employed in industry, doing dangerous work. Being small, they could move about in and under machines. This led to many accidents when they lost arms or legs, while others would be killed outright. Machines like rolling mills in the ironworks were never guarded. Luckily, the high birth rate meant that there was always another child to take the place of those injured!

Children also worked as chimney sweeps. They would be pushed up chimneys to clean them. The average survival of a child chimney sweep in the job was seven months!

Drugs!

Although more widespread in England, it was also a custom to drug children to make them more co-operative. A dose of 'Quietness' or Syrup of Poppies (a form of opium) would ensure a quiet child that would not wake you during the night or stop you working during the day.

Cholera

This would attack the throat and was spread by dirty water and infected food.

The death rate from cholera in Merthyr:

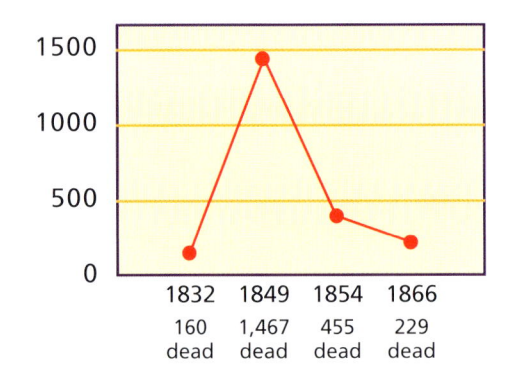

1832	1849	1854	1866
160 dead	1,467 dead	455 dead	229 dead

Charlotte Guest, wife of John Guest who owned the Dowlais Ironworks, kept a diary and noted the coming of cholera to Merthyr and Dowlais.

31 May 1849: The cholera has broken out with great violence in Cardiff. John has been to a meeting about cleaning the town. Dowlais is to be whitewashed and cleaned as much as possible. The doctors have set up a system of house to house visits to check if anyone has the early symptoms

9 June: The cholera is still raging, and has crept gradually to Gellifaelog, just across the river from Dowlais.

11 June: A letter from Dr White reports the first case of cholera in Dowlais. People are so alarmed and frightened that many imagine symptoms that are not there. The doctors will be worn out before the cholera sets in.

22 June: The cholera is worse in Dowlais – 13 deaths a day. I have sent asking for more help.

31 July: The children and I are now in the country. The cholera at Dowlais is so bad – 20 or more dying a day – eight men constantly employed in coffin-making.

'Baby Graves', a cartoon by J. M. Staniforth in the Western Mail, showing the effect of cholera.

TASK

Children died for many reasons. Some of these were to do with ignorance (the parents did not know any better at that time). Some died because at that time there was no solution to the problem (they did not then understand how to avoid some problems), but some died when there was something that could have been done then. Look at the list of reasons for children's deaths given here, and sort them into three groups – ignorance, no solution, could have been prevented.

Reasons for death:
Exhaustion after working long hours
Overdose of Syrup of Poppies
Cholera
Drinking contaminated water
Accident in a rolling mill
Baby eating same food as parents
Typhoid
Working in damp and dark conditions from an early age

Think!
What laws could have been passed to help reduce the number of children and young people who died?

In the 1840s changes were beginning to take place:

Mines Act, 1842.
No child under 10 to work in mines. Who would have supported this act? Who would have been against it?

Ten Hours Act, 1847.
People under 18 to work no more than ten hours a day.

Public Health Act, 1848.
Town councils were given powers to provide fresh water and build sewers.

A turning point?

Wales changed a great deal in the first half of the nineteenth century and as a result the lives of many people who lived there changed, too.

We have looked at this period through the imaginary experience of Daniel Jenkins and members of his family.

Think!
Going back to the start of the chapter, what do you think were the major turning points in Daniel's life? Choose four or five.

Now, compare Daniel's life in Merthyr with his life in Amlwch.

Many of these changes may have been good, others may have made his life worse.

Daniel and the Jenkins family were fictitious people but their stories were similar to the real experiences of thousands of people in Wales during this period. This is why this period is considered by many to be a turning point in Welsh history. Do you agree?

TASK

By 1850, Daniel would have been over fifty years old. You have now reached the final page of the biography of the Jenkins family. Fill in the last page by writing answers to these questions:

- What were the greatest changes that Daniel had seen since his early days in Amlwch?
- What were the best things that changed in his lifetime?
- In what ways were things worse in 1850 compared with his life in 1800?
- What change affected his life the most?
- What was the biggest turning point in his life?

2.3 Were the Welsh people troublemakers in the nineteenth century?

Look at these three famous pictures of events in Wales in the 1830s and 1840s. You may have seen them before.

In one picture the people are soaking a white flag in the blood of a dead calf, in another they are breaking down gates and in the third people are being attacked by soldiers.

Think!
What impression do the pictures give of Wales and the Welsh at this time?

In this chapter we will try to answer the following questions.

- What made people behave in this way?
- Were these people troublemakers?
- Did the behaviour of these people help to make changes in the lives of all people in the nineteenth century?
- Did the behaviour of these people help to make changes that affect our lives today?

Protesters at Hirwaun, near Merthyr, in 1831.

Rebecca Rioters at a tollgate at Efailwen, 1842.

The attack of the Chartists on the Westgate Hotel, Newport, 1839.

How do events in the nineteenth century fit into my life?

Very often today we see and hear people protesting about different issues. A quick look at the daily newspapers will give you an idea of the different issues that make people come together to protest.

TASK

Bring some newspapers to school, and cut out all the examples you can find of protests or of people protesting. Create a collage and be prepared to explain your findings to others. Remember to explain what is happening, how people are protesting and why.

Think!
Can you identify what the people in the pictures above are protesting about?

People in the twenty-first century use different methods to show that they are unhappy. They might contact a politician who could help them, or they may try to gain public support through the media.

TASK

There are many different ways in which we can give our opinion and voice our concerns. Try to identify the different methods used by people when protesting. Completing the following table will help:

Method of protesting	Possible benefits	Modern example
Letter to MP	He/she can talk to people	Local road scheme

Today, people in every part of Wales have someone who can listen to problems and who can represent us at all levels.

> Local level:
> **local councillors**
>
> Wales:
> **Assembly Members (AMs)**
>
> Britain:
> **Members of Parliament (MPs)**
>
> Europe:
> **Members of the European Parliament (MEPs)**

All these bodies – local councils, the National Assembly for Wales, the Parliament for the whole of Britain at Westminster, and the European Parliament – contribute to the way that modern Wales is governed. People decide who should represent them in regular elections. These elections play an important part in shaping the future of Wales.

Think!
Can you name the people who represent your area at each level?

When an election takes place in Wales, all who live in Wales, who are over 18 years of age, are allowed to vote. By doing this they influence how your life and your country are being governed. Politicians try to persuade you to vote for them, and on election day you enter your choice or choices on a ballot paper and then place the paper in the ballot box.

A. Field (W Party)	
C. Farmer (X Party)	
E. Shepherd (Y Party)	X
G. Bull (Z Party)	

Think!
Return to the pictures at the start of this chapter. They are all about protests. Discuss with your teacher which modern methods of protest the people in the pictures could not use. Why do you think they did not have these means of protesting?

Think!
Can you think of other methods of voting that are being used or could be used today?

Why were many people unhappy in the 1830s and 1840s?

Many people had plenty of reasons to be unhappy with life in the nineteenth century. These could sometimes combine to make an explosive mixture.

Social · **Political** · **Economic** · **Cultural and Religious** · **BANG!**

Key words

trade unions: associations of workers in order to negotiate about wages, hours and conditions
tithes: a tax paid to the Church of England
workhouse: a building where very poor people were housed and were forced to work.
independent: free from control by other countries (here, the British government and king)
republic: a country governed without a king or queen

These three pages have been designed for use as a card-sorting exercise. They can be photocopied and made up into cards.

TASK

On the next three pages, you can see many of the causes of unrest in Wales. Put these reasons into categories (some will fit into more than one category, so you will need to choose one).

➤ **Political:** about rights and freedoms

➤ **Social:** about living conditions

➤ **Economic:** about work, wages and prices

➤ **Cultural and religious:** about people's beliefs and morals

Discuss your findings with your teacher

The government was run by rich men who owned the land, factories, coal mines and iron furnaces. The ordinary people believed that the government was ignoring the problems of working people.

Many people in Wales began to think about rights and freedoms as a result of the revolution in America. In 1783 the Americans defeated their British rulers. They became an independent republic, the United States of America. Their Declaration of Independence stated that all men should be free and equal. Ideas from America spread to Wales, and the Radicals who were against the British government began to campaign for more rights and greater equality.

Key word

Radicals: people who campaigned for change

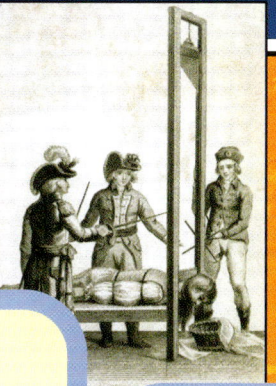

The ideas of the French Revolution of 1793 spread to Wales. In 1793 the common people of France overthrew the King and started to rid the country of the rich landowners by beheading them with the guillotine. The ideas of the French revolutionaries, 'Freedom, equality and brotherhood', were popular amongst many people in Wales.

Radicals, who disagreed with the government, sold newspapers and printed pamphlets telling people to stand up for better conditions. Radical ideas spread quickly in Wales. Between 1797 and 1815, however, Britain was at war with revolutionary France, led by Napoleon Bonaparte. These years were difficult for the Radicals: their pamphlets were banned and speaking against the government could mean prison. The Radicals did not become very active again until the war ended in 1815. Then they began again to campaign for greater equality in the voting system.

David Williams, a Welsh Radical from Caerphilly, went to Paris and was made an honorary citizen of the French Republic. He was in Paris when the French King, Louis XVI, was tried and executed.

Trade unions made people think more about how their working lives could be improved if they had more rights. During the war against France (1797–1815), it was made illegal for workers in Britain to join trade unions because the government was worried about the possibility that British workers might start a revolution.

Sometimes the employers were not able to sell their goods. When this happened they sacked workers or reduced their wages.

Old people, widows, orphans, disabled people and the unemployed had to go and live in workhouses. These were large, dismal buildings that looked like prisons. Families were separated from each other.

Some ironmasters paid their workers with tokens instead of money. The workers had to use the tokens at the shop owned by the ironmaster. This 'truck system' was unfair because prices were higher in the truck shops.

If the workers went into debt at the truck shop, the debtors' court would take family possessions to pay back the money.

Paying tithes (taxes to the Church of England) was very unpopular in Wales, especially since a large number of people went to chapels (instead of churches belonging to the Church of England).

In some Welsh chapels, ministers supported the Radicals and encouraged protest.

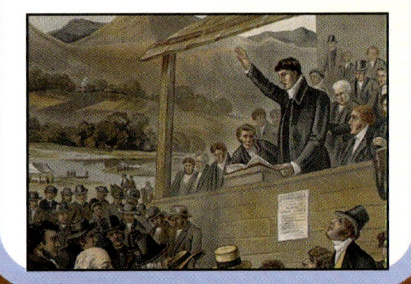

Drinking alcohol was widespread. Men would often drink to forget their miserable lives. Working in hot conditions in the coal mines and ironworks increased their thirst!

Safety at work was ignored by the owners. Machines were unguarded in factories, furnaces were extremely hot, miners underground faced danger from rock-falls, gas explosions and floods, and quarrymen worked on high and steep rock-faces. Accidents were frequent and often fatal.

Getting to work by 5 a.m. and working until 6 p.m. was not uncommon. Workers felt that they had to work hard for very little money.

Workers' housing was overcrowded, unhealthy and lacking in basic facilities like clean water and sewerage.

Wages were low in most jobs and many workers had to live in houses that they rented from their employers.

Workers had no right to vote. They had no MPs who would stand up for them and had no legal way of protesting against unfair treatment. They turned to violent action because they had no other way of protesting.

TASK

Look again at these causes of unhappiness. Discuss with a partner the five causes that you think would cause most unrest.

Why did workers think that having the vote would improve their lives?

What was wrong with the voting system in the early nineteenth century?

Working people in Wales were not allowed to vote at the beginning of the nineteenth century. Only the rich and the well-off tenant farmers were allowed to vote. However, even for those who had the vote it was not always easy to vote for the person of their choice.

Look at the cartoon and read the three sources A, B and C.

Source A
A letter to an MP, explaining the cost of an election:

The whole number that voted for you amounted to 641. Lord Mansel arranged the payment of 216 men. The Duke of Beaufort 125 men and Lord Windsor 300 men. The whole cost of buying these votes was £2,500 which amounted to £3.18s a man.

Source B
A modern historian, John Simkin, in his book *Wales in Industrial Britain*:

Bribing voters was very expensive. In 1796 John George Phillips spent £64,000 in an effort to win the Carmarthenshire seat. In 1802, William Paxton, a London banker, tried to become MP for Carmarthen. To help him win the seat he gave people who voted for him a ticket that could be exchanged for drinks in the local taverns; the bill added up to over £15,000. A landowner might warn tenants that they would be evicted if they did not vote for his candidate. Shopkeepers, solicitors and doctors were threatened with an organized boycott of their businesses if they did not do as they were told.

Key words
secret ballot: voting on paper so that others do not know how a person has voted
evict: throw out a tenant from a house or farm
boycott: refuse to have anything to do with someone because of their beliefs or actions
borough: town in the nineteenth century which had the right to send MPs to Parliament

Source C
- Wales had 27 Members of Parliament in 1800.
- Only wealthy men could become MPs.
- MPs were not paid a wage.
- MPs represented boroughs or counties. Many boroughs were former towns that had lost population and some were merely tiny villages.
- Many large industrial towns or cities had no MPs.
- Only about 15 per cent of men could actually vote (and no women).
- There was no secret ballot – voting was open and in public, so other voters knew exactly how people had voted.

TASK

1. How does information in sources A and B support what can be seen in the cartoon?
2. a) How do the sources help to explain why there was a need for a secret ballot?
   b) Why do you think that some people wanted MPs to be paid?
   c) At the time the Radicals were thought to be very revolutionary when they demanded equality for all men. Would we support their idea of equality today?
3. How are elections today different from what can be seen in the sources? Create a table to answer this question.

	1830	Today
Who votes		
Who could be MPs		
Way of voting		
Persuading people to vote for a particular candidate		
Number of MPs		
Wages of MPs		

Flashpoints of protest

There were many protests which helped to change society in Wales in the nineteenth century. Before we look at these, let us create a 'mini-book' which we shall use to write down information that we collect about these events and changes.

TASK

1. Make a mini-book of 8 pages out of one sheet of A3 paper. Insert headings on each page as shown here:

(Mini-book cover) Protests in the Nineteenth Century	1 Why people protested	2 The Merthyr Rising	3 The Rebecca Riots
4 Chartism	5a Religious disagreements 5b The 1868 election	6 The struggle for workers' rights	7 Were the Welsh people trouble-makers?

Imagine that you are writing the book for someone younger than yourself. It is important that you make your book as colourful and as simple as possible so that it can be understood.

Your book is to be called **Protests in the Nineteenth Century**. Making a suitable cover to go on the first page of your book will be your last task because you do not yet have all the information about the topic.

2. Using information that you have already from pages 124–8, complete page 1 of your book under the heading **'Why people protested'**. Use pictures as well as words. We shall complete pages 2–7 as we go on, so keep your mini-book handy and safe.

We are going to look at some events that took place in Wales from 1830 to 1868.

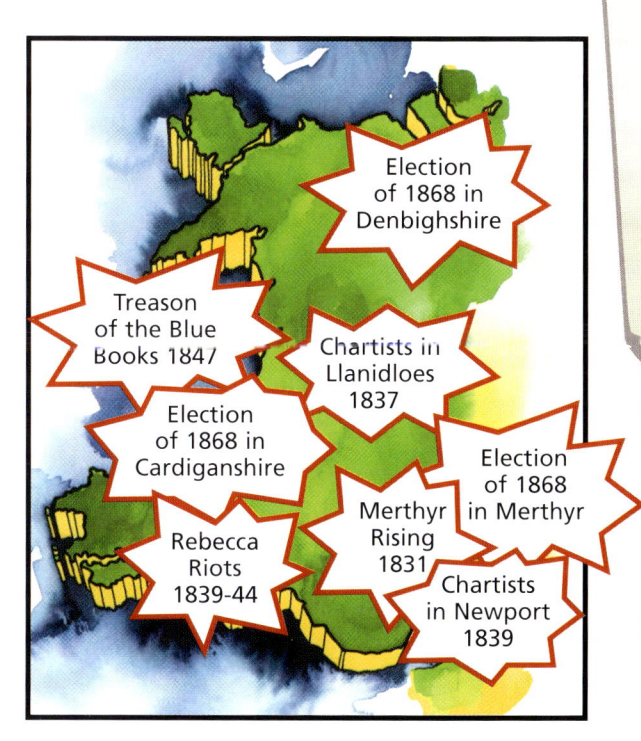

- Election of 1868 in Denbighshire
- Treason of the Blue Books 1847
- Chartists in Llanidloes 1837
- Election of 1868 in Cardiganshire
- Election of 1868 in Merthyr
- Merthyr Rising 1831
- Rebecca Riots 1839–44
- Chartists in Newport 1839

TASK

Look at the events on the map. These were times when there were flashpoints in various parts of Wales during the nineteenth century. Create a timeline to show the order in which these events occurred.

The Merthyr Rising

> **Key word**
>
> **Court of Assize:** law court where a judge hears cases
> **rising:** organized, usually armed, protest or fighting against the government

30 May 1831:
Up to 10,000 industrial workers gathered in protest on the Waun, a hillside near Merthyr Tydfil. They were angry. Why?

- In 1830 ironmasters in Merthyr reduced the workers' wages because sales of iron were lower than expected.
- In 1830 there was a big campaign in Merthyr to abolish the truck system (see page 125).
- Many people were in debt and the debtors' court had taken away some of their possessions.
- In April 1831 there was a campaign across Britain to change the law and make the voting system fairer. A Radical leader in Merthyr, Thomas Llewellyn, was arrested. He was released after 3,000 people had surrounded the prison.
- In May 1831 the ironmasters reduced wages again.

2 June:
A large crowd attacked the house of Joseph Coffin, president of the local Court of Assize. They seized the court records and burned them in the street. They dragged all the furniture out of his house and burned that, too.

Later in the day, J. B. Bruce, the local Justice of the Peace, took over the Castle Inn. He created 70 new constables and sent for reinforcements.

Think!
Why do you think Coffin's house was attacked? Why did the protesters want to destroy the records? Why do you think they burned Coffin's furniture?

3 June:
Soldiers from the 93rd Highlanders arrived at the Castle Inn. Hours later, armed with guns and bayonets, they were facing an angry crowd of 10,000 workers.

One of the workers, Lewis Lewis, called 'Away with their guns!', and the crowd charged. In the battle that followed 16 soldiers were wounded and 24 protesters died.

The Castle Inn in the centre of Merthyr Tydfil in the 1830s.

Key word

transportation: punishment for criminals by shipping them to America or Australia to do hard labour

Read the following short extracts about the events of 3 June:

'The few brave Highlanders succeeded in putting the rioters to flight. Major Falls was most severely cut about the head, and was covered in blood . . .'

'Women, screaming terrifically, searched for their husbands. A mother carried the body of her dead son in her arms. The soldiers would not permit any other of the killed and wounded to be removed.'

Think!
These two accounts give different points of view about the soldiers. Why? Which account do you think was written by William Crawshay, an ironmaster? Why?

6 June:
An armed force of 450 soldiers faced another crowd of protesters. Remembering the deaths of 3 June, the protesters returned to their homes.

7–12 June:
The people of Merthyr treated their wounded and buried their dead. Soldiers searched their homes and arrested 28 people.

13 June, the trial of Dic Penderyn:
Two of those arrested, Lewis Lewis and Richard Lewis (known as Dic Penderyn) were charged with wounding a soldier called Donald Black, with intent to kill. They were found guilty and were sentenced to death. After an appeal Lewis Lewis had his sentence changed to transportation, but Richard Lewis had his appeal turned down.

13 August:
Richard Lewis was taken from his cell in Cardiff gaol to St Mary Street where a makeshift scaffold had been built. He was hanged.

Many people believe that Dic Penderyn was wrongly executed. For many he became a martyr for Welsh working people.

Results
The Merthyr Rising had one good result. The truck system was made illegal in 1832. One of the other demands of the Merthyr protesters was for change to the voting system. In 1832 a Parliamentary Reform Bill was passed. However, there was only a small increase in the number of voters. Workers were very disappointed.

TASK

You are now in a position to write a summary about the Merthyr Rising on page 2 of your mini-book by answering these questions:

2 The Merthyr Rising

What were the causes of the protest?

What happened?

Did anything change as a result of the Merthyr Rising?

The Rebecca Riots

Modern tollgate at the Severn Bridge over the River Severn, near Chepstow in Monmouthshire.

> **Key word**
> **Nonconformists:** Protestants who refused to be part of the Church of England but had their own chapels, mainly Methodist, Congregationalist, Presbyterian and Baptist.

What were the problems facing the tenant farmers and farm labourers of Wales?

- Turnpike trusts were set up to collect tolls from travellers. This money would pay for the repair and upkeep of roads but the tolls were very unpopular. Tolls made getting to market and back expensive for local farmers who might have to pass many tollgates on the way.

- Wages of farm labourers were poor and this, combined with some years of bad harvests, caused many to worry about feeding their families.

- Rents for tenant farmers were high at this time.

- Radical pamphlets were popular and stirred up interest in ideas about equality and freedom.

- People feared the poor laws. If you wanted help you had to go to a workhouse, and treatment there was not much better than in prisons. The workhouse at Carmarthen became a prime target for the rioters.

- The Nonconformist chapels were strong in west Wales and many farmers and labourers went to the chapels and not to the Church of England services. They still had to pay the tithe (a tax to the Church) and this was resented. Most saw the English Church as supporting the English landowners who owned most of the land. The chapel ministers would often urge them to take steps to improve their lives.

The riots

When Carmarthen turnpike trust owner, Thomas Bullin, raised prices at his tollgates, farmers reacted angrily and violently, destroying tollgates in the Carmarthenshire area.

The tollgates were an easy target for protesting farmers between 1839 and 1843. Smashing them became a way of showing the anger, they felt towards many of the things they were unhappy about.

The leader called himself 'Rebecca'. He would ride a white horse and call the angry crowd to arms late at night. With torches burning and howls of anger, the tollgates of the area were attacked.

The authorities were never able to stop the attacks, despite offering huge rewards for the capture of any rioters. Even soldiers sent to the area found catching the rioters difficult.

The riots lasted from 1839 until 1843. In 1843 a tollgate keeper at Hendy, near Pontarddulais, was killed in an attack. Three men were arrested, tried and transported for their part in the riots. You can see a letter from them above.

The attacks on tollgates came to an end. At the same time the government ordered the number of tollgates to be reduced and that all tollgates should have the same rates, with a reduction for farm vehicles. In some respects the rioters had won their argument, but many of the problems still remained.

Think!

Look again at this famous cartoon of the rioters which is on p. 121. What does the cartoon tell you about
- the causes of the riots
- what the rioters were wearing
- what happened during the riots.
- How reliable is the cartoon?

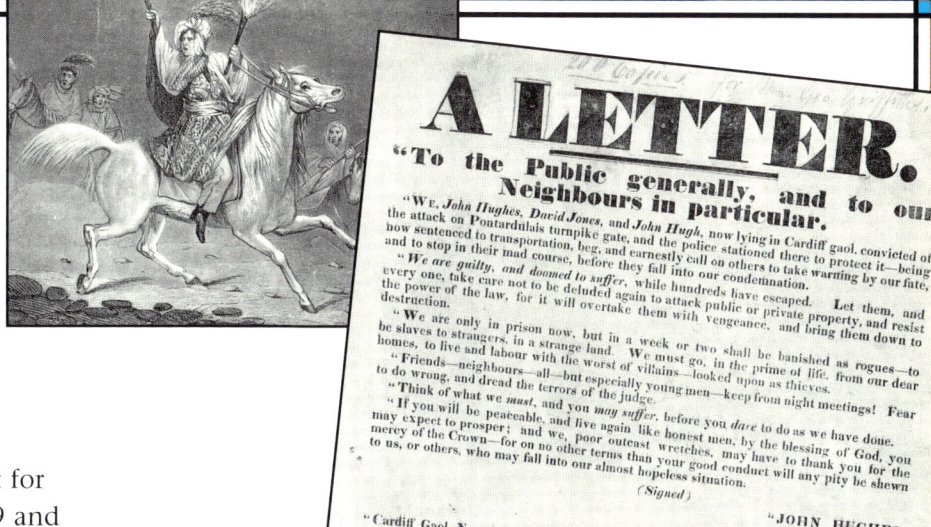

Why did they dress up as women?

This has often been debated by historians. It is likely that the need for a disguise was an important factor – the punishments for being caught were harsh. It is also possible that they took their name from a verse about Rebecca in the Bible which would have been known to many.

TASK

1. Why did the rioters attack toll-gates?
2. Why did they also attack
   a) the workhouse in Carmarthen
   b) the homes and property of landlords
   c) the homes and property of Church of England clergymen?
3. Why do you think that the soldiers found it so difficult to track down the ringleaders of the Rebecca rioters?
4. Looking at the causes of the Rebecca Riots, can you find any similarities between the causes of this protest and the causes of the Merthyr Uprising?

TASK

You are now in a position to write your page on **The Rebecca Riots** in your mini-book (page 3). Do you think the rioters were hooligans, or did they have a good cause?

The Chartists

- Parliamentary elections every year
- Votes for all men over 21
- MPs to be paid
- No need for MPs to own property
- Secret ballot
- Each MP to represent the same number of people

The six points made in the 'People's Charter'

Key words

charter: a document listing rights and demands

petition: a written demand to the government for action, signed by many people

The Working Men's Association produced a charter, containing a list of six changes they thought would lead to workers having a better life. They encouraged people to write their names on a petition supporting the points in the charter. This became known as the 'People's Charter' and, when the government refused to accept it, some of the Chartists decided to take the protests a step further.

The mid Wales disturbances

The first meeting of the Chartists in Newtown took place in April 1837. People came together to complain about the dreaded poor law which forced poor people to go to the poor house to seek help. They were addressed by a leading Chartist from Birmingham called Henry Hetherington. Hetherington had come to believe that peaceful protests would not achieve the Charter and he began to support violence as a way of forcing the government to take the petitions seriously.

Arms were handed out in Llanidloes, and the Chartists attacked some constables from London who had been sent to keep the peace. The constables were beaten up by a crowd consisting of young workers and women.

On 3 May troops arrived in the town to restore order. Over the next few weeks 32 alleged members of the Chartists were arrested.

Although no firm evidence existed against these people, all were found guilty and sentenced to long periods of imprisonment or transportation. The authorities hoped that they had killed off the movement but they were very wrong.

The Newport Rising

The date of 3 November was earmarked as the day for an attack on Newport! The plan was to take the town and send a signal out to other Chartists across Britain to do the same. It was hoped that 20,000 men would march on Newport but in the end only 5,000 men turned up. It did not help that they had to march through torrential rain. The Chartists met near Stow Hill at the edge of town and proceeded to march into the town and towards the Westgate Hotel.

This engraving by W. Taylor shows the Westgate Hotel at Newport after the attack. What evidence of the attack can you see?

The town mayor, Thomas Phillips, had already received warning of the attack, and, as the crowd drew nearer the hotel, 30 soldiers appeared in the windows of the Westgate Hotel. Volleys of shots were fired by the soldiers and the crowd had little choice but to run for their lives, leaving dead and wounded people all around (see the picture on p. 121).

Over the next few days the leaders were rounded up. In court, leaders like John Frost made passionate speeches for political change but, in spite of the judge's plea for leniency, the jury found all men guilty of treason, a charge which carried the death sentence.

After appeal the punishment was changed to transportation, and John Frost spent the next fifteen years in Tasmania as a prisoner. He eventually returned to Wales and received a hero's welcome. A statue to him was built in Newport and remains there to this day.

John Frost

TASK

1 The Chartists had six main points as shown in the picture opposite. Make a table to show what these points were and why the Chartists thought they were necessary.

2 The Chartists are often referred to as 'men ahead of their time'. What does this mean? Think about voting and Parliament today.

3 Imagine that you have been asked to produce a 'People's Charter' to improve life in Wales today. In groups of two or three draw up a list of points and give your reasons why you think they are important.

TASK

You are now on page 4 of your mini-book, '**Chartism**'. Explain the six points of the Charter, what the Chartists did, what they achieved, and why it is important to remember the Chartists.

Religious disagreements

In Welsh schools today we are taught about different religions around the world, and the emphasis is always on tolerance and understanding.

This was not the case in Wales during the first half of the nineteenth century. The Anglican Church (the Church of England) collected tithes (taxes to the Church) from everyone, whether or not they went to church. Nonconformists – mainly Methodists, Congregationalists, Presbyterians and Baptists who did not wish to be part of the Church of England – had very few rights.

By 1851 nearly 70 per cent of the people who attended church or chapel in Wales were Nonconformists.

Nonconformists also objected to sending their children to schools run by the Church of England where they might be taught Anglican beliefs. These schools were mainly English speaking. As a result the Nonconformists struggled to build their own schools and organized Sunday schools.

Above, the church at Carew, Pembrokeshire, belonging to the Church of England (now Church in Wales), and, below, Mydroilyn chapel, Cardiganshire, a Nonconformist chapel.

The Treason of the Blue Books

The battle between the Church of England and the Nonconformists increased after 1847. The main reason for this was a report published in that year about the state of education in Wales.

Government inspectors questioned witnesses and visited schools throughout Wales, but their work was heavily influenced by the fact that 80 per cent of those they questioned were members of the Church of England. The investigations were carried out almost entirely in English.

Think!
Why do you think people thought the inspectors might be unfair?

Key word

perjury: lying on oath

The resulting report criticized education in Wales but also said that the morals and ignorance of the Welsh were appalling. Here are some extracts from some people who gave their opinions to the inspectors:

Source A

The morals of the Welsh people are totally corrupt and abandoned. The common people herd like beasts.

Source B

Perjury is common in courts of justice, and the Welsh language makes this easier.

Source C

The men and women, married as well as single, live in the same house and sleep in the same room. The men do not hesitate to wash themselves naked before the women; the women do not hesitate to change their under-garments before the men.

Think!
- Why do you think people giving evidence to the inspectors would make these comments about the Welsh?
- How do you think many Welsh people would feel about these comments? Why?

This report was seen as an attack on Wales and came to be known as 'the Treason of the Blue Books'. There was uproar in Wales as the Nonconformists rushed to defend Wales, Welsh morals and the Welsh language.

The divisions between the Nonconformists and the Church of England increased. These spilled over into politics. There were two main political parties called the Liberal Party and the Conservative Party (or Tories). The Tories were the party of the landowning class. The Nonconformists supported the Liberals.

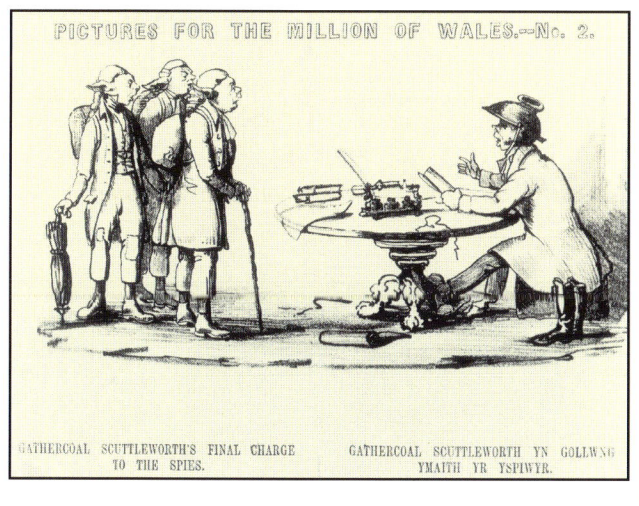

A cartoon by Hugh Hughes intended for a Welsh audience shows the commissioners being instructed by the Secretary to the Committee on Education, Sir James Kay-Shuttleworth. What impression was the cartoonist trying to give?

TASK

On page 5 of your mini-book, under the heading **'Religious disagreements'**, write down in half a page the reasons why the Nonconformists disliked the Church of England.

The 1868 election and the secret ballot

Key word

Act: a law made in Parliament

The 1867 Reform Act

Throughout the nineteenth century there were campaigns to increase the number of people allowed to vote in elections. In 1867 a major reform took place. The number of voters in Wales was almost doubled. In the early 1860s there were 62,000 voters in Wales. After 1867 there were 121,000.

Background

Before 1868 all Wales's MPs had been wealthy landowners who were mostly Conservatives (Tories), but the election of 1868 broke the mould as Wales returned Liberals to the House of Commons. Wales was represented by 21 Liberals and only 12 Conservatives.

The Liberals supported the rights of Nonconformists and claimed to represent the ordinary people of Wales, not the landlords.

Merthyr

There was a great Liberal victory in Merthyr where the Nonconformist minister Henry Richard defeated a local landowner.

Denbighshire

In Denbighshire there was a famous victory for the Liberal candidate, George Osborne Morgan.

The Tory backlash

Following the election of 1868 many landowners were very unhappy at the way their tenants had voted. Voting was open then, and it was easy for the landowner on stage to see who, during a show of hands, had not supported him. As a result of the election many tenant farmers were evicted from their farms. In 1868 43 farmers were evicted from their farms in Cardiganshire, 26 in Carmarthenshire, while 80 workers from the Penrhyn quarry lost their jobs.

The secret ballot

Henry Richard and George Osborne Morgan criticized the landowners in Parliament and led the campaign to get the secret ballot made law. They were finally successful in 1872 when the Secret Ballot Act was passed. Voters could now use their vote without fear of being victimized.

The year 1868 was a turning point in Welsh history. Wales now had people in Parliament who were in a better position to speak for the ordinary people of Wales and could present their problems in Parliament.

TASK

On the second half of page 5 in your mini-book, '**The 1868 election**', explain how the 1868 election changed politics in Wales. Why were the election and its results so important in our history?

What happened after 1868?

Mass protest meeting of workers at Merthyr, 1875.

Things did not improve overnight for working people after the changes in the voting system. The protests about working conditions in particular continued. Industrial unrest became a feature of Welsh life during the next forty or so years, as we can see from the events listed here and on the next page.

- **1871 and 1875**
  Long and bitter disputes in the south Wales coalfield

- **1874**
  The North Wales Quarrymen's Union formed at Caernarfon

- **1884**
  All men over 21 given the vote

- **1885**
  Miners' leader William Abraham ('Mabon') elected Liberal MP for the Rhondda

- **1887**
  The 'Tithe War' broke out in north-east Wales when farmers refused to pay the tithe to the Church. Violence followed when the government sent in troops to stamp out the protests.

- **1893**
  290 men died in Cilfynydd coal mine disaster

- **1898**
  The South Wales Miners' Federation formed

- **1900**
  Strike by the members of the Amalgamated Society of Railway Workers, Taff Vale

A strike poster at the time of the Taff Vale Railway Strike in 1900

- **1900–3**

    Penrhyn Quarry strike. A three-year strike of slate workers against the demands of quarry owner Lord Penrhyn. It became the longest strike in British history

- **1900**

    Keir Hardie elected as MP for Merthyr Tydfil, the first MP for the Independent Labour Party which was gaining more and more support from Welsh workers

- **1910–11**

    Riots at Tonypandy by striking miners

- **1911**

    Rail strike at Llanelli where 2 men were shot by troops

- **1913**

    Senghennydd mining disaster – 419 miners killed

The Strike Defence Committee of the Penrhyn strikers in 1903. This formal photograph shows them in their best clothes.

TASK

1 From looking at the list, what do you think many workers felt about their working conditions? What did they do to try to improve them?

2 Choose one of the events closest to your school. Using your IT skills, find out about it and write a short history of that event:

    What were the causes of the event? Briefly explain what happened. What, if anything, changed as a result of this event?

    Produce your work on 3 sides of A4 paper with pictures and explanations.

3 On page 6 of your mini-book, fill in your summary of '**The struggle for workers' rights**'. How did workers try to improve their working conditions?

TURNING POINT

1868 –
A turning point in Welsh history?

After 1868 Welsh people became more involved in important political issues, and they also struggled for better conditions and more rights at work. Industrial unrest often led to strikes, the forming of trade unions and workers becoming more militant. By 1914, the workers' dissatisfaction with many issues led to growing support for a new political party, the Labour Party.

But the majority of Welsh people still supported the Liberal Party in 1914. It was not until after the First World War (1914–18) that the Labour Party began to grow strong throughout Britain.

Key word

militant: actively determined to demand change

TASK

1. You have now reached the last page of your mini-book. Can you remember the title of this page, **'Were the Welsh people trouble-makers in the nineteenth century?'** Now is your chance to write your opinion. Use the last page to answer the question.

2. Your mini-book is still not finished. The front cover has to be completed. Create a cover that reflects the story that you have written

Miners waiting to go into a mass meeting at Tonypandy, November 1910, during the Cambrian Combine strike.

2.4 How was Wales changing at the start of the twentieth century?

Cardiff at the start of the twentieth century

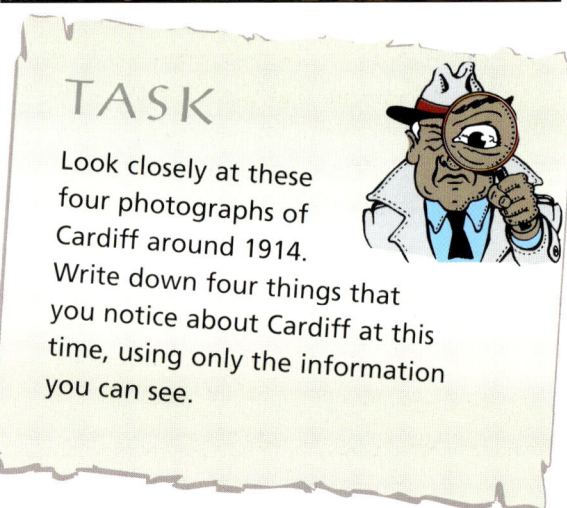

TASK

Look closely at these four photographs of Cardiff around 1914. Write down four things that you notice about Cardiff at this time, using only the information you can see.

You have seen four pictures of Cardiff around 1914. Now read the following extract that was printed in the newspaper, the *Western Mail*, on 1 January 1914:

It is interesting to take a look at the Cardiff of the early 1870s as compared with the Cardiff of today. The first and best measure of our progress is the growth of population. Today the inhabitants of the city of Cardiff are estimated to number 182,000; in 1871 they numbered 47,500. In trade, our coal shipments in 1871 totalled 2,979,000 tons; in 1912, 10,102,700 tons. Wages are far above those in the 1870s. Colleges and schools, libraries and parks, churches and chapels, telegraphs, telephones, and postal facilities, shops, and transport within the city and to all parts of our own and other countries have added to the comforts of life. They could not have dreamed of such progress in the 1870s.

The years between 1870 and 1914 were not only years of great change for Cardiff; they were years of great change for the whole of Wales. In this section we shall look at four of these great changes. These changes can be described as 'turning points' because each one was of such significance that they help us to understand the Wales in which we live today.

1 Wales increased its population by over 1 million. A lot of this increase occurred in south-east Wales, which is still the most heavily populated area of Wales today.

2 The majority of workers worked in heavy industry, such as coal-mining, steel-making, tinplate-making, slate-quarrying, building and dock labour. This trend continued until the 1970s. Many of the towns and villages that people live in today were built around coal mines, steelworks and docks.

3 There was a big change in what people did in their leisure time. Many of these leisure activities are still with us today, such as sporting activities like rugby, going to the cinema, and going to the beach.

4 Because of the increase in population, in particular of those speaking English, the percentage of people speaking Welsh in Wales declined to below 50 per cent by 1914. The downward trend in the numbers speaking the language continued for most of the twentieth century, but there was a slight rise towards the end. Most people in Wales before 1914 still considered themselves to be Welsh, and there was a greater public awareness of Welsh history and Welshness amongst both English- and Welsh-speakers.

TASK

1 Make a list of the changes in Cardiff between 1870 and 1914 that you can suggest from reading this passage. Use the following headings: population; coal exports; communications; leisure facilities; education; travel.

2 Look back at the photographs. What evidence can be found to support the points in the passage?

1. The change in population

Between 1871 and 1911 the population of Wales grew by over 40 per cent. It increased from 1,412,883 to 2,420,921. There were over a million more people living in Wales at the end of this period of forty years, 1871–1911.

The population of Wales 1871–1911

(Graph: 1871: 1,413,000 → 1911: 2,421,000)

The population of some counties of Wales 1801–1911

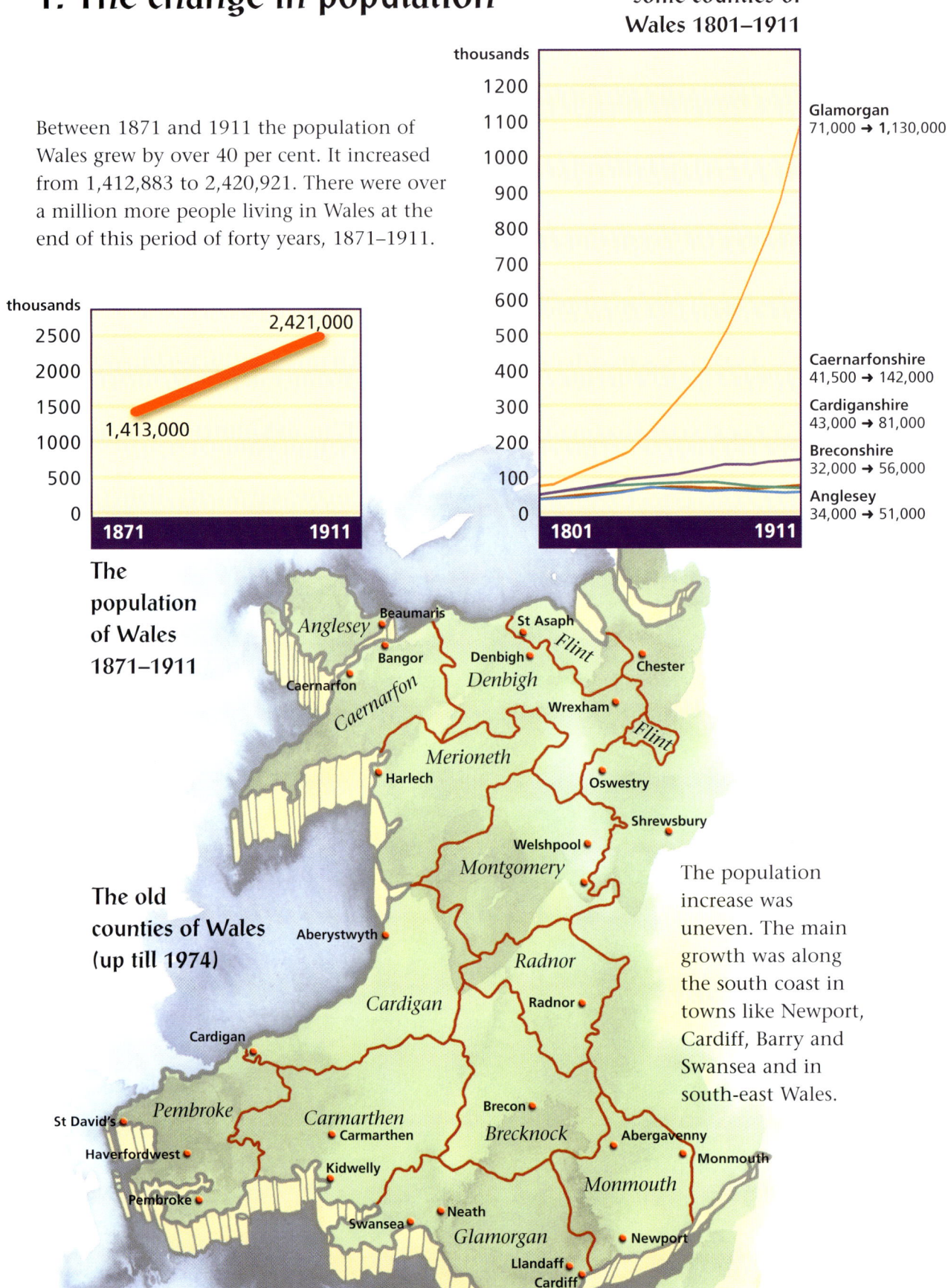

- Glamorgan: 71,000 → 1,130,000
- Caernarfonshire: 41,500 → 142,000
- Cardiganshire: 43,000 → 81,000
- Breconshire: 32,000 → 56,000
- Anglesey: 34,000 → 51,000

The old counties of Wales (up till 1974)

Counties shown: Anglesey, Caernarfon, Denbigh, Flint, Merioneth, Montgomery, Cardigan, Radnor, Pembroke, Carmarthen, Brecknock, Glamorgan, Monmouth

Towns shown: Beaumaris, St Asaph, Bangor, Denbigh, Chester, Caernarfon, Wrexham, Harlech, Oswestry, Shrewsbury, Welshpool, Aberystwyth, Radnor, Cardigan, St David's, Haverfordwest, Pembroke, Carmarthen, Kidwelly, Brecon, Abergavenny, Monmouth, Swansea, Neath, Llandaff, Cardiff, Newport

The population increase was uneven. The main growth was along the south coast in towns like Newport, Cardiff, Barry and Swansea and in south-east Wales.

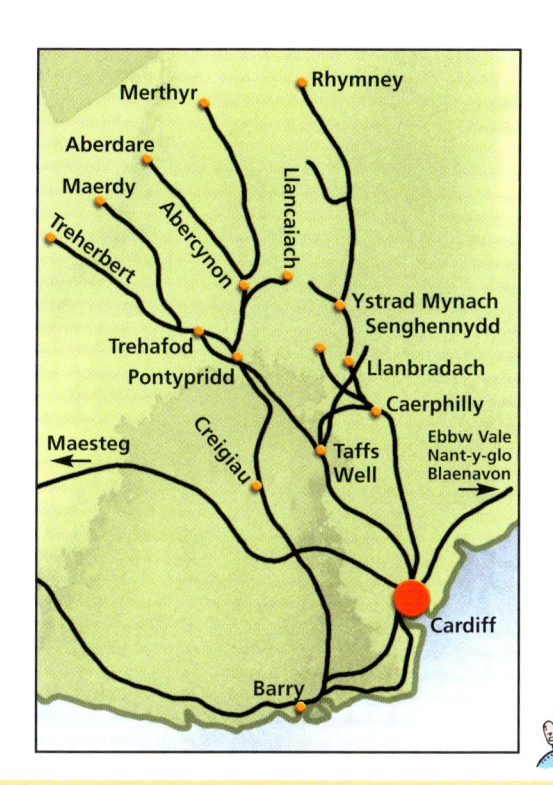

Key words

immigrant: person moving into an area from another area or country
rural: of the countryside

If you travel to Cardiff by train from places such as Rhymney, Merthyr Tydfil, Aberdare, Maerdy, Treherbert, Pontypridd or Maesteg, you travel on the 'Valleys Lines'. The 'Valleys' is a term used to describe a large part of the south Wales coalfield. This is the area in which towns and villages grew into existence, almost overnight, between 1870 and 1914, with the growth of the coal industry.

Communities with a rich mix of people developed. Immigrants came into the area from other parts of Wales – rural north Wales (such as the old county of Caernarfonshire), mid Wales (such as Breconshire), and from rural west Wales (such as Cardiganshire). They also came from counties in England such as Herefordshire, Gloucestershire and Somerset. Many also came from Ireland and further afield.

By 1901 one-third of the population of Wales lived within a 25-mile radius of Cardiff. By 1911 55 per cent lived in the former county of Glamorgan. The main reason for this major change was the growth of the coal industry, in particular in the Rhondda Valleys.

Even as late as 1841, the Rhondda Valleys contained quiet farming communities and had a population of less than 1,000.

In 1853, the first large coal mine was sunk, and within three years a railway line had been built to transport the coal. From then on, development of many coal mines was rapid. Within 20 years the population there grew to 24,000.

Rhondda coal won recognition as the best steam coal in the world and was exported through Cardiff, Barry and Penarth docks all over the world. By 1914, the population of the Rhondda was about 153,000.

This photograph of the Rhondda Valley was taken in 1900. It shows the Glamorgan Colliery at Llwynypia in full production.

TASK

Look back at the graph on page 144 which shows the rise in the population of Wales in the period 1871–1911. This shows a population increase of 1 million. The graph is very useful because it gives us an idea about the massive scale of the population change. What it does not tell us is the story behind the growth in population. The growth in population set off a chain reaction. Once people started coming to work in the newly opened pits, what did they need? Think about houses, services, leisure time, transport, and so on. Create a spider diagram like the one below, filling in the boxes with what people needed.

Areas where population grew:
- south-east Wales, because of coal-mining, iron and then steel-making, and transport of coal for export, especially through the ports of Cardiff, Barry and Penarth.
- north-east Wales, especially Denbighshire and Flintshire, which also had coal and steel industries
- north-west Wales, because of the demand for slate for roofing, fireplaces and window sills.

Areas where population declined:
- Rural north, west and mid Wales where agriculture remained the main source of work, such as Anglesey, Breconshire, Cardiganshire or Montgomeryshire. Many people born in these areas would spend their lives outside the county of their birth.

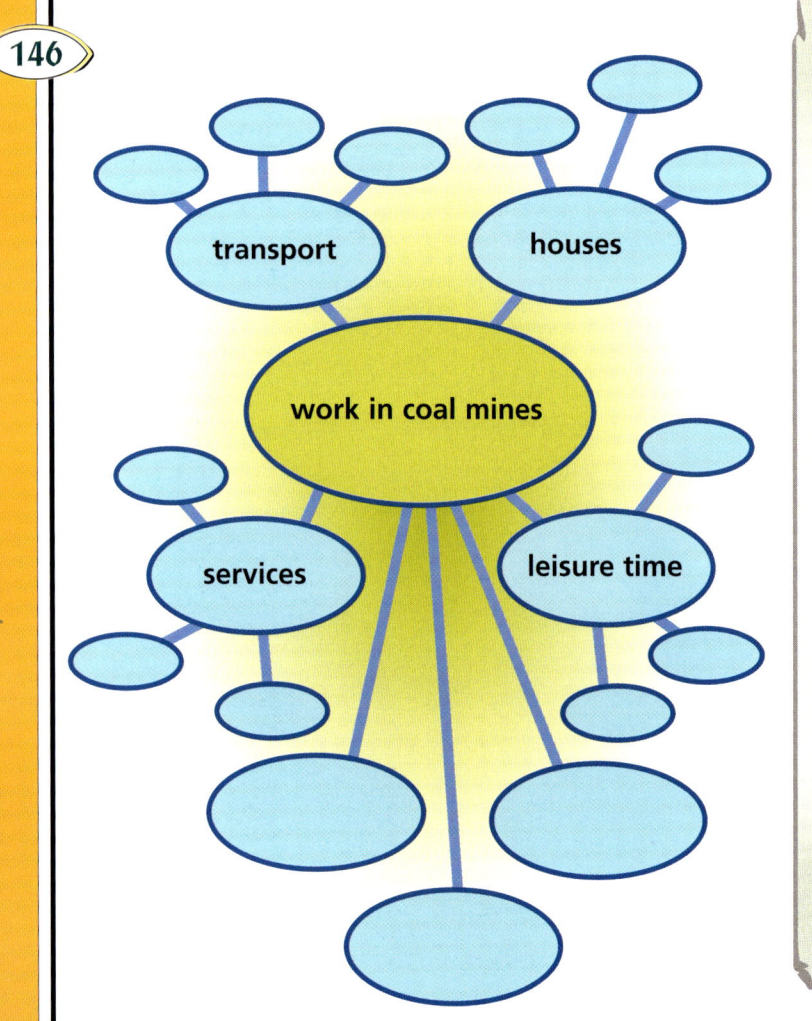

TASK

Look again at the graph of population of some Welsh counties on page 144.
1. What kind of counties – rural or industrial – were Breconshire and Cardiganshire by about 1911?
2. In 1871 there were more females than males living in Wales (706,535 females as compared with 706,048 males). In 1914 there were 965 females for every 1,000 males. Can you think of reasons why this change took place?
3. There were different male/female ratios in different counties in Wales. Look at the figures below and discuss with a partner possible reasons why there was such a difference between Cardiganshire and the Rhondda in 1891:

	Men		Women
Rhondda	1,314	for every 1,000 women
Cardiganshire	776	for every 1,000 women

Wales outside Wales

Key word
drapery: a shop selling cloth (and clothes)

Many Welsh people left Wales in search of work and a better life during the nineteenth century, though by 1900 the rate of emigration was low because Wales was booming. In 1900 about 265,000 people born in Wales were living in England.

There was a large Welsh community in London. Since Tudor times the Welsh had been flocking to London as the capital of government and a place where they could make money. By the end of the nineteenth century there were about 35,500 Welsh-born people in London, double the figure of 1851. The Welsh became especially noted for their dairies and milk rounds in London, and then for their numerous drapery stores. Some of their stores became household names, like Peter Jones of Sloane Square, D. H. Evans of Oxford Street, Dickens and Jones of Regent Street.

Other areas of settlement in England were the Midlands, and especially in Liverpool. Liverpool was regarded by some as the capital of north Wales.

Peter Jones came to London from Carmarthen in 1871 and opened a drapery shop. Then he opened this large store in Sloane Square, London. By 1890 he employed 300 people, most of them from south-west Wales.

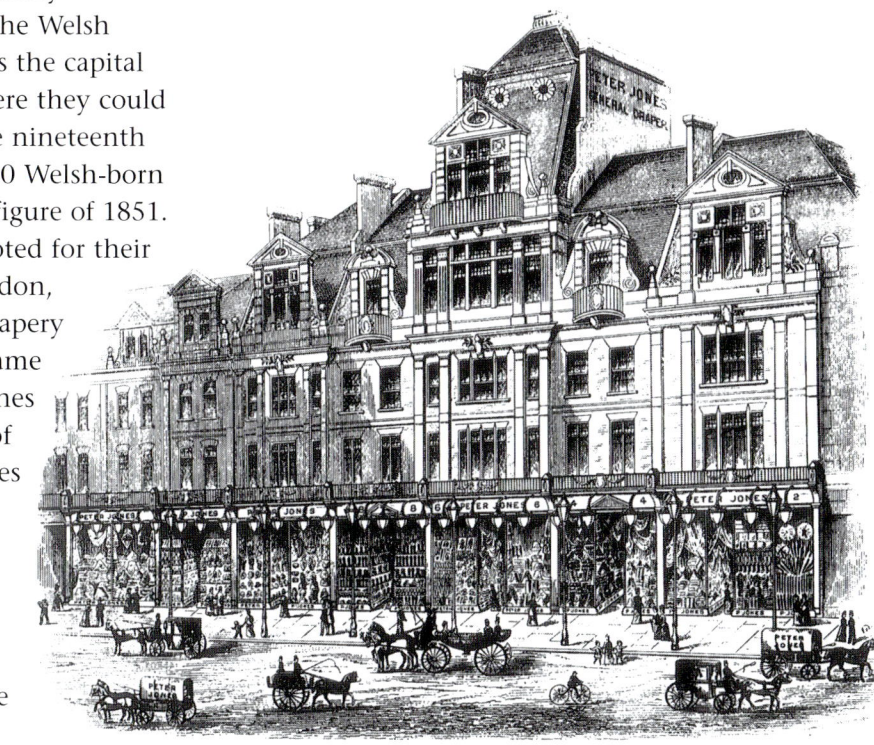

Fitzclarence Street Calvinistic Methodist Welsh Church, Liverpool, in 1885.

The greatest concentration of Welsh people abroad was in the United States of America. It was estimated in 1890 that just over 100,000 people born in Wales were then living in America. Many settled in the ironworks towns of Scranton and Wilkes-Barre in Pennsylvania. In 1872 there were 384 Welsh-language chapels in the USA. The connection remains strong today.

Scranton, Pennsylvania, USA, held an annual eisteddfod but by the end of the nineteenth century this had developed into an international music festival held in the English language.

A drawing of the choral competition at the Scranton Eisteddfod of 1880.

Another 200,000 Welsh people lived overseas in Australia, New Zealand, Canada and South Africa.

An intermediate school in the Chubut Valley, Patagonia, with children of Welsh settlers, 1908.

There was a small but strong Welsh community in Patagonia, a part of Argentina. The original group sailed there from Liverpool on the ship *Mimosa* in 1865 and settled in the Chubut valley, where other emigrants from Wales later joined them. In spite of great hardships the community survived, and many of their descendants today still speak Welsh, as well as the official language of Argentina, Spanish.

Think!
Welsh people emigrated for many reasons.
- Why was London so popular?
- Why was Liverpool a magnet for people from north Wales?
- Why did places like Scranton in the USA attract emigrants?
- Why were countries like Australia, New Zealand, Canada and South Africa a focus for emigration?
- The emigrants who went to Patagonia had special reasons for sailing to an isolated part of South America. Can you work out why?

2. Changes in work

In 1913, 234,134 men were employed in the coal industry in Wales. This was equivalent to one-tenth or 10 per cent of the total population. This figure alone should give an impression of how important coal-mining was in Wales.

The majority of male workers in Wales in 1881 were employed in one of the following industries:
- coal
- steel
- tinplate
- slate
- transport (railways and docks)
- agriculture

Between 1881 and 1911 the numbers employed in all these, except agriculture, increased significantly. In agriculture the numbers fell.

Towns and villages were built around and close to pits, quarries, steelworks, tinplate works, docks and railway engineering centres. They provided homes and facilities for the workers and their families. As a result many of the houses and buildings in our towns and villages today date back to the last years of the nineteenth century and the early years of the twentieth century.

Think!
Discuss with a partner the older buildings in your village, town or city, such as chapels, cinemas, workmen's halls, factories and so on. Make a list of those that you think were built in the years between 1870 and 1914. Create a class list. Discuss the reasons why they were built and what they are used for today. What can buildings tell us about changes in the last hundred years?

Bethesda, a slate town in north-west Wales

Housing built for mine workers at Chirk, north-east Wales.

As the large towns developed, work in the service and retail industries increased too.

Key words

service industry: companies providing services to people rather than goods, for example, banking, insurance
retail industry: shops selling goods
domestic service: work as a servant in another person's house

A general store at Bethesda.

The heavy industries did not provide much work for women after the industrial reform acts prevented women from working in coal mines. The service and retail industries provided some opportunity for women to find employment. Over half the women in paid employment, however, were in domestic service (servants).

Women were also, of course, the largest unpaid workforce in the land. Women houseworkers faced daily the endless task of shopping, feeding, cleaning and washing without the help of the machines that we have today.

Think!

What does the *Bennett's Business Directory* for Port Dinorwic in north-west Wales tell you about the shops and services available to people in a town at this time?

North Wales   Port Dinorwic.
Bennett's Business Directory
PORT DINORWIC

BANKERS: – Lloyds Bank. North & South Wales Bank. London City and Midland Bank.
CHURCH: – St. Mary's. Vicar, Rev. J. T. Jones, B.A.
COUNTY COURT: –Held at Carnarvon.
EARLY CLOSING DAY: – Thursday.
POPULATION: – 2,700.
POSTAL: – A money order and telegraph office under Bangor: postal deliveries, 7 a.m. and 4 p.m.
PUBLIC BUILDINGS: – Working Men's Conservative Club.
RAILWAYS: – The station is on the Bangor and Afon Wen branch of the London and North Western Railway.
REGISTRAR OF BIRTHS AND DEATHS: – J. R. Jones
SITUATION: – In the county of Carnarvon, on the shore of the Menai Straits, 5 miles south-west of Bangor, and 4 miles north-east of Carnarvon.
TRADE: – Slate quarrying.

Banks H M, cycle agent, Bangor st
Caddock W, Tea Rooms, 73 Bangor st
Davies J, grocer, Bangor st
Dinorwic Slate Quarries
Edwards E, grocer, Cinallt, Snowdon st
Edwards H, surgeon, Bangor st
Edwards J, grocer, Anchor House, Snowdon st
Edwards Mrs, grocer, Menai Hill
Eifl Commercial Hotel, 76 Bangor st
Evans D, grocer, Dinorwic house
Evans H, draper, Snowdon st
Evans T, grocer, Bangor st
Foulkes J R & Co., ship, yacht, and boat, builders, Dinas.
Francis T, taxidermist, Bangor st
Garddfon Inn, Beach Row
Griffith E, boot and shoe establishment, Bangor st
Horlock W, fish frier, 60 Bangor st

Throughout this period, people's work experiences had a lot in common, whether they were working in a coal mine, in a steelworks, in a slate quarry, in the docks or in the home.

1. Work took up a lot of people's time.
   - The working day was long – often 10–12 hours.
   - The working week was long – Sunday was the only full day off. Most people worked until at least midday or 2 p.m. on Saturdays.
   - The only holidays were bank holidays.

2. Most people's work involved hard manual labour. This often meant:
   - Hard physical labour – lifting, carrying, using heavy tools, and so on.
   - Dirty and uncomfortable working conditions.
   - Working in extremes of temperature, either hot or cold.
   - Working with the ever present fear of accidents.
   - Working in conditions that were unhealthy and could lead to disease and death.

TASK

On this and the following page you will see pictures of miners working. Using the bullet points from point 2 above as headings, and using examples from the evidence of these pictures, write a sentence on each bullet point to give a more detailed account of a miner's work. You can start your first sentence like this: Miners' work was hard. For example, they had to . . .

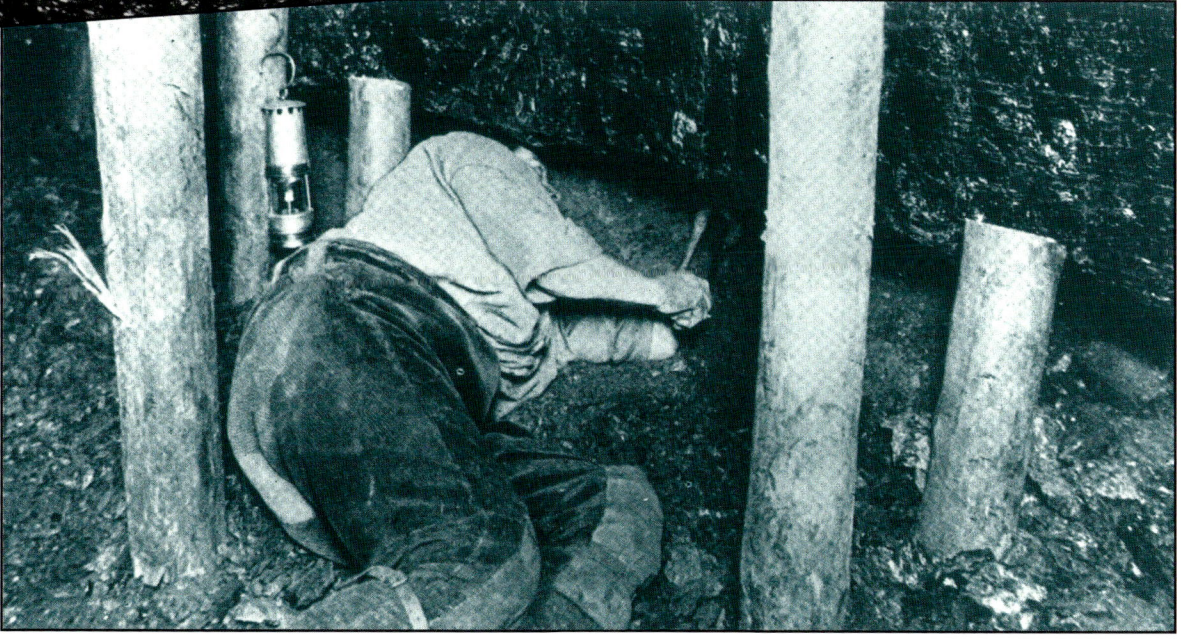

Funeral of some of the victims of the disaster at Darren Colliery, Deri, Bargoed, in 1909.

TASK

Read this extract about a woman's life in the Rhondda and look at the pictures below. Using the same bullet points that you used to describe a miner's work, describe the work of a miner's wife.

Key word

go to service: become a domestic servant

I am a native of Cardiff and went to service up the Rhondda where I had a brother working, and it was there I met my husband, who was a miner. I was thirteen when we married in 1903. As a town-bred girl I found the life very different from what I had been used to. I was very shocked that we had nowhere for our husbands to bath in. We had to bring a tub or tin bath, whichever we had, into the same room that we lived in, and heat the water over our living-room fire in a bucket or iron boiler. So you can imagine the life of a miner's wife is no bed of roses. We have to do our weekly wash in the same room, so that our one room was not much to look at. By the time we had done our daily clean, it was looking all right, until Hubby came home. Then after he had bathed and his clothes put to dry, and turned from time to time, there is a nice film of coal dust all over the room, and it means you want the duster in your hand continually.

Also we have no boilers, or coppers I should say, to boil our clothes in. We have to boil them over the living-room fire. No wonder so many little children are scalded to death in Wales, as many people, unthinking, put the hot water in the bath first, forgetful of the little ones toddling around them, and they stumble into it. A little one, living close by me, five years old, died last week through falling in a bath of boiling water that was being prepared for his father to bath.

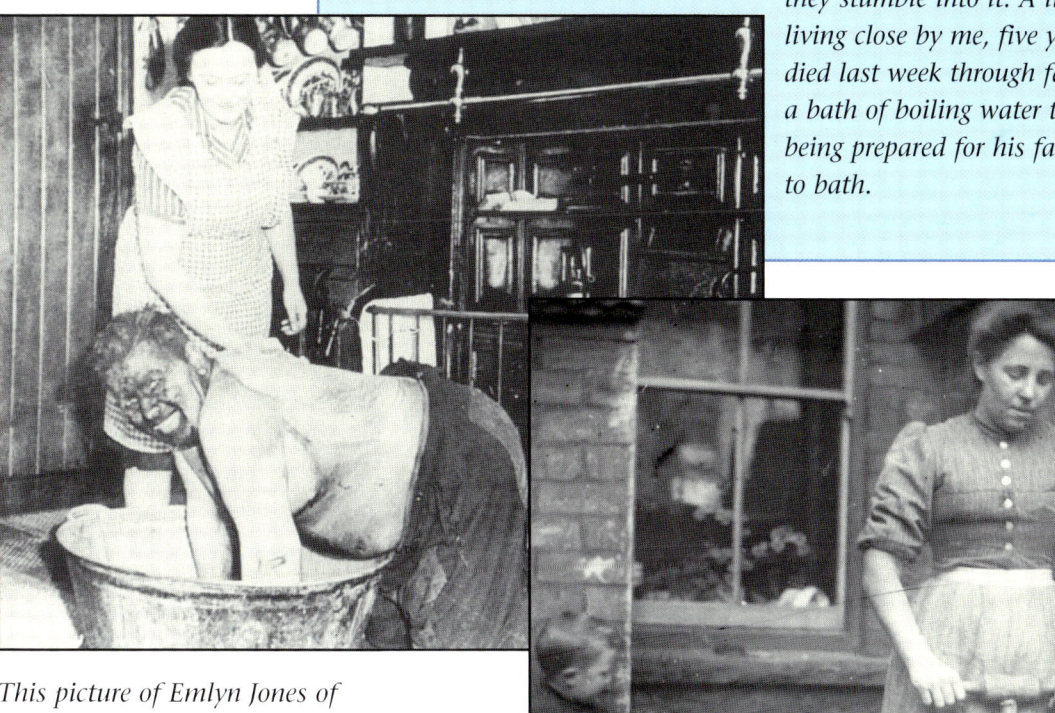

This picture of Emlyn Jones of Tynewydd, south Wales, having his back scrubbed by his wife Agnes was actually taken in about 1948.

3. Changes in leisure activities

Key word

Band of Hope: children's society to promote temperance (keeping away from alcohol)

Although working and living conditions were harsh for the working classes, there is plenty of evidence that they lived life to the full and made the most of their leisure time. They enjoyed taking part in activities that involved a lot of people, for example, choirs, bands and team sports.

Evan Roberts, the famous revivalist preacher, with his assistants.

Chapels and churches

Most of the large villages and towns had a number of chapels and at least one church. These buildings were often the largest buildings in a street. In 1905 over half a million people belonged to a chapel.

At times, Wales would go through a religious revival. This is an awakening of religious feeling in large numbers of people at the same time. One such revival began in 1904, when a minister from Loughor near Swansea, Evan Roberts, said that God had come to him. Many people, especially young people, felt the same and soon the word spread and thousands of people joined in revival meetings and services.

The chapels and churches were full on Sundays. People dressed in their 'Sunday best' clothes and went to services in which they sang, listened to Bible stories and prayed together.

On Monday, like the previous Sunday, an overflow meeting was held outside the chapel because of the size of the audience. There were many ministers in this meeting. Some of them had come from far away to see and judge for themselves whether the message had come from the heavens or from man. Crowds of people would ask me 'Is is true?' I was sure that it was.

(T. Francis, Nonconformist and revivalist minister from Gorseinon, writing in 1906)

The revival had a strange effect on me. My friends and I would play prayer meeting. Lavinia and I pretended to sing hymns while Oswald would close his eyes and pray. There was one boy who wanted his cat saved, so we saved his cat with a mixture of singing and praying in front of our amused parents. On Mondays our parents would go to prayer meetings while we played.

(Annie Miles from Pontrhydyfen remembering 1905 in an interview in 1996)

The chapels especially organized a lot more than religious services. There were events organized every evening and often at weekends. Tea parties were arranged for children, there were choir practices, brass band practices, drama societies and many other activities. Children went to the Band of Hope and to Sunday schools. In the summer, the Sunday school trips and Whit walks were very popular with the children.

Many of the chapels were Welsh-language chapels. They organized their own eisteddfods at which people sang, read poetry, played musical instruments and performed amateur dramatics.

Tabernacle Wesleyan Sunday School, Treorchy, about to start their Whit walk through the town in 1914.

> *Our social life was all around the chapel. And it wasn't dull, mind. We had an awful lot of fun.*
>
> (Woman from Llwynypia, Rhondda, remembering the start of the twentieth century)

TASK

For many families life outside work or school revolved around the chapel or church. Using the description of chapels and churches and the illustrations, fill in some church/chapel activities for a family on this imaginary calendar for a Whitsun week.

	Father	Mother	Child
Sunday			
Monday			
Tuesday			
Wednesday			
Thursday			
Friday			
Saturday			

No one would be doing an activity every day. On some days more than one activity might take place.

TABERNACLE BAPTIST CHAPEL, PONTYPOOL.

THE ANNUAL TEA PARTY

OF THE ABOVE CHURCH WILL BE HELD

On Thursday, August the 29th, 1872;

Tea on the Table at Three o'clock. Tickets, 1s. each.

If the weather is favourable, the Tea will be provided in Penygarn Field—if wet, in the Tabernacle Chapel.

A PUBLIC MEETING

AT SEVEN O'CLOCK.

Part of the annual Corpus Christi procession of Roman Catholic schoolchildren in Cardiff in 1911.

Public houses

For every chapel in a town, there was a place that sold alcohol. Public houses (pubs) were often rough places which only men went to. There was sawdust on the floor and spittoons on the bar.

Beer was a great thirst-quencher for men, for many spent their days doing manual work in hot conditions.

Some of the bars were in workingmen's institutes. Here there were billiards rooms, cards and domino tables, concert halls and libraries. In the early twentieth century they were to become the first 'picture houses' showing silent films.

Key word
temperance: keeping away from alcohol
spittoon: bowl to spit into

Miners enjoying a drink after their shift at Cwmbach, Aberdare, about 1910.

An early travelling cinema at Pwllheli.

> *In all Llanelli had a ratio of one public house per 179 people, but it must be remembered that public houses were a perfectly ordinary part of everyday life, providing thousands of ordinary people with food and drink.*
>
> (Russell Davies in his book *Secret Sins: Carmarthenshire, 1870–1920*)

In the 1870s the best-known choir came from Aberdare. It was founded by a blacksmith called Griffith Rhys Jones from Abercynon. Everyone knew him as Caradog. In July 1873 he entered his 500-strong choir for a competition at the Crystal Palace in London against the best choirs in England. As many as 20,000 people came to listen to the final rehearsal at Caerphilly Castle.
   Caradog's choir won a great victory and returned to Wales with the first prize. There were amazing scenes when the choir returned home. There were crowds at Cardiff station and a massive welcome when they finally got home to Aberdare.

'The Land of Song'

Choirs were popular throughout Wales in the second half of the nineteenth century. Some were all male and some were mixed.

By the end of the century most towns and villages had at least one choir and numerous competitions were held up and down the country. The choirs were followed by fans everywhere they sang. It was like supporting a football team today.

Many towns and chapels had orchestras or bands as well as choirs.

> *An English visitor to the National Eisteddfod at Merthyr Tydfil in 1881 commented:*
>
> *Six choirs entered the choral competition with a total of 1,456 voices. It took three hours to hear these six choirs sing. During all this time the vast audience remained standing.*

The beating of the 'All-Blacks'

From the 1880s there was a growth in sport as a popular pastime – both to play and to watch. Football was the sport of the working classes and remained popular. In England, rugby football was played mainly by rich public-school boys. In Wales, however, it caught the imagination and large numbers of rugby clubs were founded. By 1900 the Welsh had earned a reputation for being skilful rugby players. Between 1900 and 1912 Wales won the Triple Crown (that is, the team beat England, Ireland and Scotland) six times.

The greatest day of all, however, was on 16 December 1905. Wales played the New Zealand 'All-Blacks'. They were the best rugby team in the world and many thought them unbeatable.

A crowd of 47,000 packed Cardiff Arms Park to watch a Welsh team including miners, tinplate workers and boilermakers. The Welsh won the match and Wales became famous for its rugby team.

Carmarthenshire people do not say a lot about religion. They are sometimes excited by political disagreements. But in none of these matters of late years has there been anything like the interest which was taken in the football [rugby] match between Wales and New Zealand. Business almost stopped to wait for the telegrams. The result produced scenes as yet unrivalled.

(*Carmarthen Weekly Reporter*, a local newspaper in Carmarthenshire, 22 December 1905)

The Welsh rugby team that beat New Zealand in 1905.

Boxing was another popular working-class sport. Jim Driscoll from Cardiff on his knees against Freddie Welsh from Pontypridd in 1910. These Welshmen were two giants of British boxing at that time and were famous in Europe and America.

TASK

Compare the following sport and leisure activities at the start of the twentieth century with the same activities today. What has stayed the same? What has changed? Why do you think the changes have taken place?

- Public houses
- Cinemas
- Musical activities
- Sport

4. The Welsh language and culture

Key word

depopulation: fall in the number of people living in an area

This period was a crucial one in the history of the Welsh language. In the early nineteenth century it is believed that approximately 80 per cent of the population spoke Welsh. The census of 1891 was the first one to ask people to record information about the language they spoke. Here are the percentage figures for those speaking Welsh recorded for 1891, 1901 and 1911:

1891	54.4%
1901	49.9%
1911	43.5%

By the end of the nineteenth century, therefore, a slight majority of people living in Wales could not speak the native language. Because of the increase in population, however, the actual numbers speaking the language had not decreased a huge amount.

Janet Davies, the author of a book on the Welsh language, has described this change as being of 'momentous importance'. She continues: *Until the twentieth century it was possible to define the Welsh people as a people who were mainly Welsh speaking. That definition was no longer true.*

The downward trend in the numbers speaking Welsh continued in the twentieth century but increased slightly by the end of the twentieth century.

1931	36.8%
1951	28.9%
1981	18.7%
2001	20.5%

The national figures did not show that there were great variations across Wales. In most of north-west and south-west Wales, Welsh was still the language of the vast majority of people. But these were the same areas where depopulation was occurring. In the new, expanding, industrial south-east, the decline was far greater than the national figures show.

I only spoke Welsh with my parents, but I would play in the street with the children of incomers. I became more accustomed to English. My father was very angry when I began to answer him in English but my mother said: 'Leave him be, it doesn't matter. Anyway he needs to get ahead in life.'

Jack Jones writing about his childhood in the Rhondda between 1900 and 1914 in *Unfinished Journey* (1938).

As soon as I spoke Welsh everyone laughed and a string was put around my neck with a heavy wooden token tied to it. I had put a similar device around the neck of a dog to stop it running after sheep.

O. M. Edwards, writing in 1897.

Language difficulties have all but vanished in south Wales where parents have taught their children the value of English. The same effort must now be made in north Wales.

A School Commissioner, writing in 1895.

TASK

How do these quotations help to explain why the Welsh language declined during the nineteenth century?

Bontnewydd Council School, Caernarfonshire, about 1905. Note the portraits of the king and queen on the wall. After 1880 it was compulsory for all children to attend primary schools in Wales. The language of the classroom was English. In 1907 O. M. Edwards became the Chief Inspector of Schools. He encouraged teaching in schools through the medium of Welsh in areas where Welsh was the first language.

Look at the quotations. Why do you think O. M. Edwards felt strongly about this?

Think!

1. 'In 1911 there were more people in Wales who could speak Welsh than ever before, or since.' Look at the statistics on page 158. How could this be true?

2. Between 1891 and 1911 the number of Welsh speakers in Anglesey, Caernarvonshire, Carmarthenshire, Cardiganshire and Merioneth was between 89% and 95% of their populations. In 1911 58% of the population of Glamorgan could only speak English. Explain why you think that there was such a difference.

3. Can you think of any reasons to explain why, for the first time since the number of Welsh speakers in Wales was recorded in 1891, there was a percentage increase in 2001?

Although the Welsh language was in decline at that time, there was great interest in the language, culture and history of Wales during this period.

The National Eisteddfod at Chester in 1866.

- The National Eisteddfod was reorganized in 1880, and became a popular event every year in Wales.

- National teams were formed in many sports – most notably football and rugby.

- The National Library was opened in 1909 in Aberystwyth

Old College, Aberystwyth, the first college of the University of Wales, opened in 1872. The establishment of the college was paid for out of collections among working people. In 1893 colleges at Cardiff and Bangor joined with Aberystwyth to form the University of Wales.

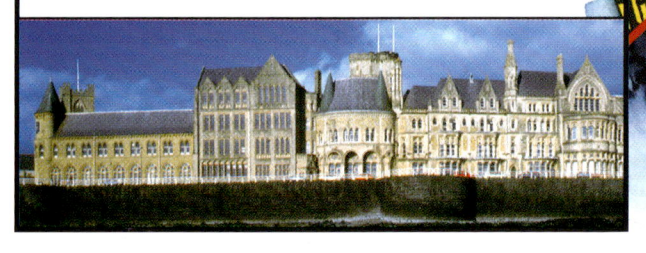

The monument in Ynysangharad Park, Pontypridd, to Evan and James James, father and son, the composers of the Welsh national anthem.

- 'Hen Wlad fy Nhadau', written and composed by Evan and James James of Pontypridd in the 1860s, became accepted as the Welsh national anthem.

- The National Museum was opened in Cardiff in 1908.
- A separate Welsh Department of Education was created in 1907.

All these national developments were taking place at a time when, for the first time, the majority of people living in Wales could not speak the Welsh language.

Being Welsh in 1914

Different parts of Wales had different experiences in the years 1870–1914. South-east Wales saw a massive increase in its population. On the other hand the island of Anglesey witnessed depopulation. North-west Wales was dominated by the fortunes of the slate industry, the area around Wrexham by the coal industry, Newtown and mid Wales by the woollen industry and agriculture, Llanelli by the tinplate industry, Cardiganshire by agriculture, south-east Wales by coal. North-west Wales was mainly Welsh-speaking whilst south-east Wales was increasingly English-speaking.

Wherever people lived and whatever their individual experiences throughout Wales there were strong feelings of community and of 'being Welsh', whether they spoke Welsh or not.

The Dowlais Temperance Choir on the steps of the Crystal Palace in London, where it won the competition for temperance choirs in 1895.

Dr Bill Jones, a historian, wrote about the people in the new industrial areas:
For many, the joys of choir singing and the thrills of the rugby game were ways to becoming Welsh.

In the industrial areas the working-class people shared similar experiences. People worked closely together in hard conditions. They lived through times when there was plenty of work and other times when there was unemployment. They lived through disasters together when people died in accidents. They lived through troubled times together when there were strikes against the employers.

They lived in close communities and shared enjoyment outside work. They watched and played sport together. They sang in, or listened to, choirs together. They took part in and attended concerts together. They went to chapel together. The men went to the pub together. Sharing these experiences helped them to identify with each other.

This chapter has looked at four ways in which Wales changed between about 1870 and 1914.

1. The change in population.
2. The growth of heavy industry.
3. The change in leisure activities.
4. The changing fortunes of the Welsh language.

TASK

At the beginning of the chapter it suggested that these four changes could be described as 'turning points' in the history of Wales. Write a paragraph on each of the changes to say whether they were a turning point or not.

Before you start, think about the reasons that an event in history might be called significant. Think about the following questions:

- Was the change important to people at the time?
- Were people's lives affected deeply by the change?
- Were a lot of people affected by the change?
- Were people's lives affected for a long time afterwards?
- Does studying these changes help us to understand the world in which we live today?

TASK

You have been asked to design a front cover for a book entitled *Changing Wales, 1870–1914*. You need to illustrate the four changes described in this chapter. What illustrations would you choose? You can choose from this book, another book or from the Internet.

Be prepared to talk about your cover and to justify your choice of illustrations.

TASK

In the Middle Ages, wealthy people used to have coats of arms. These were in the shape of shields and were divided into three sections. Each section said something about themselves and their beliefs.

Imagine that you have been asked to sum up what it meant to be Welsh at the start of the twentieth century by creating a coat of arms.

1. What would you put in each of the sections of the shield? It could be a symbol, a person, an item of clothing, a photograph of a building, a group of people, a slogan, the title or words of a song and so on.

2. Once you have chosen your three images, write a short paragraph on each to justify your interpretation so that you can report back or make a presentation to the class.

3. All class members report back to the class with their choice of images. Make a list of the different choices that have been made. Discuss them and as a class choose three images to create a class shield.

4. Create a shield that represents your own views on what it means for you, today, to be Welsh. Discuss this with other members of your class.

Glossary

Act: a law made in Parliament

ancestors: forefathers, people from whom you are descended

appointed: given a job or title

assassination: murder of an important person (often for political reasons)

Band of Hope: children's society to promote temperance (avoiding alcohol)

bard: a poet who usually sang verses and played the harp.

bilingual: speaking two languages

bishop: a leader of the Church

borough: town in the nineteenth century which had the right to send MPs to Parliament

boycott: refuse to have anything to do with someone because of their beliefs or actions

Catholic: a member of the Church of Rome under the leadership of the Pope.

census: a head count of all the people living in a country

charter: a document listing rights and demands

confess sins: tell a Catholic priest what you have done wrong

contemporary: from the time of the events

Court of Assize: law court where a judge hears cases

court: law court to hold trials, but also means the place where a ruler lives and keeps his/her servants and followers and government, e.g. the English court

depopulation: fall in the number of people living in an area

domestic service: work as a servant in another person's house

drapery: a shop selling cloth (and clothes)

dynasty: a succession of rulers of the same family

enclosure: the fencing in and claiming of land by rich landowners

enclosure acts: laws forcing the fencing off of common land to form private property

evict: throw out a tenant from a house or farm

execution: putting someone to death as a punishment

exile (live in exile): forced to live outside his own country

feuds: quarrels, often fighting, over long periods of time

gentleman: a member of the gentry

gentry: the landowning class

go to service: become a domestic servant in someone else's house

grazing: feeding cattle and other farm animals on grass growing in the field

guardian: someone who looks after a child in place of parents.

heiress: a woman who inherits a lot of money or land.

hostage: a person taken prisoner by one side in order to put pressure on the other side.

immigrant: person moving into an area from another area or country

independent: free from control by other countries

invade: attack and enter (from somewhere outside the country)

Justice of the Peace: a member of the gentry appointed to be responsible for law and order

landlords: people who own land which is rented out to tenants

landscape: what the land looks like

life expectancy: the number of years a person is likely to live

live in exile: forced to live away from the home country

martyr: someone put to death for his/her beliefs

mass: Catholic church service

militant: actively determined to demand change

minority language: language spoken by fewer people than the main language of a country

monarchs: kings and queens

mortality rate: the death rate in a particular area or period

navvies: labourers who built the canals

Nonconformists: Protestants who refused to be part of the Church of England but had their own chapels, mainly Methodists, Congregationalists, Presbyterians and Baptists

outlaw: outside the law, wanted by the law

Parliament: the law-making body of government, until the nineteenth century made up of the king with representatives of the landowning classes.

perjury: lying on oath

petition: a written demand to the government for action, signed by many people

pilgrimage: journey to a holy place

point of view: idea, opinion

prophecy: foretelling of the future

Protestant: a member of a church that broke away from the Catholic Church in the sixteenth century

Radicals: people who campaigned for change

raids: sudden attacks

Reformation: sixteenth-century movement to reform the Catholic Church, which ended with the Protestants breaking away from the Catholic Church

reign: time during which a king or queen rules a country

relics: bones or belonging of a dead holy person, thought to have special powers

republic: a country governed without a king or queen

retail industry: shops selling goods

revenge: hurt done to someone in return for a wrong or injury already suffered

rising: organized fighting against the government

rural: of the countryside

scythe: a hand tool for mowing long grass or crops

secret ballot: voting on paper so that others do not know how a person has voted

service industry: companies providing services, rather than goods, for example, insurance, banking

sheriff: official appointed by the monarch to keep law and order in each county

shrine: place of worship where saints' relics are kept

silicosis: lung disease caused by breathing in silica dust

smelting: melting ore (rock containing metal) to get the metal out

soul: moral, religious part of a person

spittoon: bowl to spit into

standard-bearer: person carrying the flag of the leader

temperance: avoiding alcohol

tithes: a tax paid to the Church of England

trade unions: associations of workers to negotiate about wages, hours and conditions

traitor: a person who betrays his/her own side

tramroads: roads with metal tracks for carts carrying coal or iron, pulled by horses

transportation: punishment for criminals by shipping them to America or Australia to do hard labour

trapper: child whose job was to open the trap-doors down a coal mine for trams carrying coal

turnpike trusts: private companies formed to build and repair roads and to collect tolls to pay for the roads

uplands: mountainous, high land

vagabond: a homeless person, a tramp

workhouse: building where very poor people were housed and forced to work

Yeomen of the Guard: the king's personal bodyguard

Notes for teachers

1. The idea of a 'turning point' in history is one of the themes of this book. To help pupils understand this idea, an exercise has been provided at the start of the book. The exercise attempts to make the concept relevant to pupils' own experience and is not specific to any historical period or topic.

2. Throughout the book the History Skills Gang icons are used to help pupils understand basic historical skills. The information about the characters is provided on pages 7–9 for reference purposes to support explanation of the skills to pupils.

3. Two chapters of the book are intended as 'big picture' exercises aiming to provide overviews of the historical periods 1485–1760 and 1760–1914. These chapters contain a large amount of historical source material, but they have been constructed as exercises introducing a limited amount of evidence at a time. It is not necessary for every pupil to engage with all the evidence.

4. The other chapters of the book are extended studies intended to provide knowledge, understanding and activities for pupils over several lessons. Suggested activities, including card-sorts, are integrated into the content but it should be possible for teachers to present the information according to their own preferred method. Further detail on each chapter is given below, and it may be useful to read this before teaching the relevant chapter.

PART 1 1485–1760

1.1 What was life in Wales like between 1485 and 1760?

The purpose of this section is to enable pupils to construct an overview of life in Wales during the period 1485–1760. It is intended that pupils gain a sense of historical period rather than viewing history as a series of unconnected events and developments.

The section is based on a selection of contemporary pictorial and written evidence. It is structured so that pupils undertake a series of tasks that introduce them progressively to historical evidence and associated issues.

It is not the intention that every pupil examines every piece of evidence. They are introduced to pictorial evidence first and to written evidence at a later stage. Initially, tasks are designed for group work with the intention that pupils become 'experts' on different themes. The strategy is designed to support the development of oracy skills through discussion and the presentation of information back to the class.

The tasks build from being observational and making lists to writing a paragraph based on a number of sources.

As well as gaining historical knowledge and understanding, pupils are introduced to factors that determine the availability of sources and their nature. They are introduced to the idea of making suggestions about the past based on available information and to how historians select and combine information from sources in order to write their own accounts.

1.2 Should Henry VII be a Welsh hero?

In this section pupils are provided with information on Henry VII's early life up until his victory at Bosworth Field. This is broken up with a series of short exercises designed to facilitate understanding and to encourage pupils' thinking and their ability to ask their own historical questions.

The second half of the section examines different points of view about Henry and what he did for Wales. It explores the reasons why George Owen, a member of the Elizabethan gentry, would have a good opinion of Henry VII and why other people have disagreed. Finally, pupils are asked to make their own judgement. The statements on p.42 may be photocopied and used in a sorting exercise.

1.3 Why was the translation of the Bible into Welsh in 1588 an important event in Welsh history?

This section seeks to explain the reasons for the translation of the Bible into Welsh in the wider context of the Reformation and events in Europe. There are a number of stages in the section.

The first part of the section explains the Reformation and developments in Wales and England up until the early years of Elizabeth's reign.

The information on pages 52 and 53 is designed for use as a card-sorting exercise and should be photocopied. The intention is to provide information on the European background to the events of 1587–1588. Teachers may wish to develop some of this information. The exercise provides background to help pupils make connections between events that took place in Wales, England and Spain in 1587.

The third stage of the section focuses more specifically on the translation of the Bible into Welsh, and why it was so important in 1588. Pupils are provided with a writing frame to help them to express their understanding.

The final stage of the section considers the reasons why the translation of the Bible was an event of significance in Welsh history and aims to give it some contemporary relevance.

PART 2 1760–1914

1.1 How did Wales change between 1760 and 1914?

The format and aim of this section are similar to those of section 1.1. Pupils are introduced to pictorial and written evidence from the period 1760–1914 in order to create an overview. They are encouraged to become 'experts' on one particular theme and understand developments within the theme during the whole period.

Within the section there is a strong focus on change, not only between the beginning and the end but also within the period.

2.2 Why was Wales on the move?

This section focuses on the early nineteenth century and how the lives of rural farmworkers were transformed when they moved to work in industrial areas. The story is told through the experiences of a fictional family, and especially one individual who leaves Anglesey and ends up living and working in Merthyr Tydfil. An overarching task throughout the chapter is the production of a biography of the leading character.

The section begins by explaining the plight of tenant farmers and labourers and goes on to examine the development of early industries. Once again a 'jigsaw' exercise is suggested whereby pupils only examine one industry in detail, but gain an overview of the other industries from listening to the outcomes of the work of other pupils.

The last part of the section concentrates on living and working in Merthyr Tydfil and asks questions about why people moved to industrial, urban areas and about the quality of life there.

2.3 Were the Welsh people troublemakers in the nineteenth century?

This section has an overarching task – the production of a mini-book that summarizes the events in the section and requires pupils to answer the 'big' question: were the Welsh people troublemakers in the nineteenth century?

The first part of this section relates the topic to the pupils' own times and is intended to support their understanding of democracy.

The exercise on pages 124–6 may be photocopied. It is anticipated that it would be best done as a card sort.

The chapter goes on to look at five major events – the Merthyr Riots, the Rebecca Riots, the Chartist Rising in Newport, the Treason of the Blue Books and the 1868 general election. There are separate exercises on each of these, so that they could be studied independently if desired.

2.4 How was Wales changing at the start of the twentieth century?

The final section examines four 'turning points' at the end of the nineteenth century and the start of the twentieth century. Pupils may consider these as independent topics, but together they build towards discussion of what it meant to be Welsh at this time, thus addressing a dimension of the Curriculum Cymreig. The question is also related to pupils' own experience.

The section concludes with an interpretations exercise, requiring pupils to select illustrations to characterize a historical period.

Index

A

Aberdare 156
Aberystwyth 160
Abraham, William ('Mabon') 139
Acts of Union 41, 62
'All Blacks' 157
American Declaration of Independence 124
Amlwch 88, 96, 97, 98, 103
Ammanford 80
Anglican Church see Church of England
Askew, Anne 47

B

Babington Plot 58
Bala 74
Bangor 106
Bargoed 152
Barmouth 99
Beaufort, Margaret 30, 34
Bersham 99
Bethesda 149, 150
Bible in Welsh 18, 53–64
Bontnewydd 159
Bosworth Field, Battle of 28, 35, 37, 39, 42
Brechfa 89
Britannia Bridge 68, 76, 95
Brittany 31
Brymbo 99

C

Cadiz 48, 54
Cadwaladr 35
Caernarfon 76, 95, 106
'Caradog' 156
Cardiff 42, 69, 71, 77, 108, 142–3, 144, 145, 155, 160
Carmarthen 33, 34, 56, 132, 133, 147

Catholics 19, 44, 45, 46, 47, 48, 49, 50, 58
Cefn Mabli 57
Chartists 65, 121, 129, 134, 135
Chepstow 20, 104
Chirk 149
Church of England 124, 134, 135, 136, 137
Cilfynydd 139
Clasemont 79
Clynnog, Morys 56
Conservative Party 137, 138
Cornwall 42, 46, 60, 61
Corwen 88
Crawshay, Richard 108
Crawshay, Rose 112–13
Crawshay, William 108, 111, 112, 131
Cyfarthfa Castle 111, 112
Cyfarthfa Ironworks 86, 108

D

Dafydd Llwyd of Mathafarn 35
Dale 33
de Mendoza, Bernardino 21, 56
Dic Penderyn (Richard Lewis) 131
Dinefwr Castle 20, 36
Dolgellau 99
Dowlais Ironworks 100, 108
Drake, Francis 54
Driscoll, Jim 157

E

Edward I, King 5
Edward IV, King 31, 32
Edward VI, King 46, 47, 50, 62
Edwards, O. M. 75, 158, 159
eisteddfod 148, 155, 160
Elizabeth I, Queen 38, 41, 45, 47, 48, 50, 51, 52, 54
Elizabeth of York 38

F

Ferndale 77
France 31, 48
French Revolution 125
Frost, John 135

G

Gaelic 60, 61
Germany 49
Glamorgan Canal 105
Glyndŵr, Owain 29, 35
Guest, John 108
Guest, Lady Charlotte 112, 118
Gwydir Castle 15
Gwyn, Richard 19, 26, 58

H

Haverfordwest 34
'Hen Wlad Fy Nhadau' 160
Henry VI, King 30, 31, 32
Henry VII, King (Henry Tudor) 8, 9, 28–42, 56, 62
Henry VIII, King 38, 41, 44, 45, 46, 50, 57
Herbert, Edward, 1st Baron of Chirbury 13, 23
Hetherington, Henry 134
Homfray, Samuel 67

I

Ireland 48, 56, 90, 95
Italy 49

J

James, Evan and James 160

K

Katherine of Valois 30
Katheryn of Berain 13

L

Labour Party 140, 141
Lancastrians 29, 30, 31, 38
Lee, Rowland 57
Lewis, Lewis 130, 131
Lewis, Richard (Dic Penderyn) 131
Liberal Party 137, 138, 139, 140, 141
Little Orme, Llandudno 55, 58
Liverpool 93, 147
Llanelli 77, 140
Llanidloes 103, 129, 134
Llannerch 16
Llanrwst 68
Llwynypia 145, 155
Llywelyn ap Gruffydd 5
London 39, 40, 48, 147
Ludlow 39
Luther, Martin 44, 49

M

'Mab Darogan' 29, 35
Mansel family 12, 24
Manx 60, 61
Mary, Queen 19, 47, 48, 50
Mary, Queen of Scots 48, 51, 53, 54, 58
Mathafarn 33, 35
Menai Bridge 76, 94, 95, 104
Merthyr Rising 121, 129, 130, 131
Merthyr Tydfil 73, 74, 82, 83, 86, 100, 105, 106, 108, 114–18, 130, 131, 138, 140, 156
Montgomery Canal 105
Morgan, George Osborne 138
Morgan, Thomas 58
Morgan, William 52, 55, 56, 59, 62
Myddleton, Sir Hugh 62

N

Napoleonic Wars 100, 102, 125
Neath 76
Netherlands 49, 51
Newport 65, 73, 121, 129, 134, 135, 144
Newport Rising 134, 135
Newtown 105, 134
Nichol, William 19, 26
Nonconformists 132, 136, 137
Northern Ireland 61

O

Owen, George 8, 14, 21, 28, 40, 41
Owen, Hugh 58

P

Parys Mountain 78, 96–8
Patagonia 148
Pembroke Castle 28, 31
Pennant, Richard (Lord Penrhyn) 93, 94
Penrhyn 70, 93, 94, 140
Philip of Spain, King 48, 53, 54, 56, 58, 60
Plas Mawr, Conwy 16
Pontrhydfendigaid 71
Pontypool 79
Pontypridd 105, 160
Pope, the 19, 44, 45, 49, 56
Port Dinorwic 150
Powys Castle 15
Princes in the Tower, the 31, 32
Protestants 19, 44–50, 58

R

Radicals 124, 125
Raglan Castle 31
'Rebecca' 132, 133
Rebecca Riots 121, 129, 132, 133
Red Bandits of Mawddwy 57

Reform Act (1832) 131
Reform Act (1867) 138
Rhondda Valleys 71, 77, 113, 115, 145, 146, 153
Rhymney 108
Rhys ap Thomas 34, 36, 39
Richard III, King 28, 31, 32, 34, 35, 36
Richard, Henry 138
Roberts, Evan 154

S

St Asaph 64
St Davids Cathedral 46
Salesbury, William 62, 63
Scotland 48, 61
Scranton, USA 148
Secret Ballot Act (1872) 138
Senghennydd 140
Shrewsbury 33, 34, 36
Spain 48, 51, 54, 56
Spanish Armada 53, 60
Stanley, Lord Thomas 34, 36, 37
Stanley, Sir William 34, 36, 37
Stephenson, George 106
Swansea 78, 98, 108, 144

T

Taff Vale Railway Strike 139
Telford, Thomas 104
'Tithe War' 139
tithes 125, 132, 139
tollgates 104, 133
Tonypandy 140
Tories see Conservative Party
Tower of London 31
translation of the Bible into Welsh 43, 50, 55, 56, 59–64
Treason of the Blue Books 137, 138
Tredegar 110
Tregaron 103, 117

Treorchy 155
Trevithick, Richard 106
truck shops 101, 125, 131
Tudor, Edmund 30
Tudor, Henry *see* Henry VII
Tudor, Jasper 30, 31, 34, 39
Tudor, Owen 30
turnpike trusts 104, 132

U
University of Wales 160
USA 124, 148

V
'Valleys' 145
Vaughan, Sir Christopher 41

W
Wars of the Roses 29, 30
Welsh, Freddie 157
Welsh language 53–64
Welshpool 105
Wesley, John 103
Whitgift, Archbishop 55, 56, 59
Wilkinson, John 99, 102
Williams, David 125
Williams, Thomas 96

Y
Yorkists 29, 31, 32, 38

Acknowledgements

Every effort has been made to contact the copyright holders of material published in this volume, but if any have been inadvertently overlooked the publishers will be pleased to make the necessary arrangements at the first opportunity.

Photographs

The publishers would like to thank the following for permission to reproduce photographs:

T = top, B = bottom, C = centre,
L = left, R = right

Cover picture: *Trefforest Tinplate Works: Pickling and Annealing*, by T. H. Thomas, 1874. By permission of the National Library of Wales.

Bodleian Library, 47T; Bridgeman Art Library, 16T, 31B; © British Coal Corporation, 149B; British Library, 60; © British Museum, 38TC, 96T; Butetown History and Arts Centre, 69B; By kind permission of the John Lewis Partnership archive collection, 147T; By permission of Pennsylvania Anthracite Heritage Museum, 148C; CADW, 5TR, 15T, 16B, 19, 31TR, 36T, 40BR; Church of St Andrews, Presteigne, 18T; Church of St Mary's, Tenby, 18BR; Courtesy of WorldWideWales.tv, 160B; The Cuneo Estate, 106T; Cyfarthfa Castle Museum & Art Gallery, 69T, 100T, 110C, 112T; ffotograff, 28T, 43; The Francis Frith Collection, 6BL; © GKN and courtesy of the Glamorgan Record Office, 112B; The Guildhall Library, Corporation of London, 40; Gwynedd Archives, 57B, 149C, 150, 156C; Harvington Hall, 58; Hulton Archive/Getty Images, 6BR, 111T, 121TL, 127; The Illustrated London News, 115, 116, 121BL; Jeremy Lowe, 114CR; © Manchester Art Gallery, 113C; Merthyr Tydfil County Borough Services, 156B, 161T; Monumental Brass Society, 30B; Museum of London Picture Library, 4; National Library of Wales, 6CL, 21, 43L, 55BL, 56, 57C, 68T, 71C, 74T, 74B, 76T, 76C, 76B, 78T, 79B, 80, 87, 88B, 94C, 95T, 95BL, 99, 100B, 102T, 102BL, 105C, 106B, 108, 109T, 113B, 114CL, 116, 125, 130, 133T, 136, 140C, 147B, 148B, 154, 156, 157B, 159, 160TR; National Motor Museum, 5B; National Museums & Galleries of Wales, 13L, 13BR, 71C, 79B, 86T, 86B, 88C, 89, 95BR, 102BR, 109C, 110B, 109B, 119, 140B, 145C, 151C, 151B, 152B, 153R, 155BL, 156T; National Portrait Gallery, 6, 30C, 31C, 33, 38TR, 38BL, 38BR, 59; National Trust Photographic Library, 20T, 93; 13TR, 94B, 20T, 20B; Newport Museum & Art Gallery, 7, 65, 73B, 121BR, 133B, 135T, 135B; Postcard of the late F. Jones, 71B; Pembrokeshire County Council, 31TL, 46T; Photolibrary Wales, 43, 122, 123; Powis Castle Trustees, 15B; Private collections, 6CR, 12, 41, 67; Royal Commission for the Ancient and Historic Monuments of Wales, 35, 64, 70; Rhondda Archive Photograph Series, 153L; Rhondda Cynon Taf Libraries, 46C, 105B; St Peter's Church, Selsey (J. Smith), 37B; Scottish National Portrait Gallery, 54; Shrewsbury Borough Museum, 36C; South Wales Argus, 132; Stewart Williams, *Cardiff Yesterday*, 142BL, 155BR; Stewart Williams, *Old Aberdare and Merthyr Tydfil in Photographs*, 111B, 112C; Stewart Williams / Cyril Batstone, *Old Rhondda in Photographs*, 145, 155C; Stowe School, Buckingham 37T; Swansea Maritime & Industrial Museum, 98; Topfoto/Fotomas, 23, 29R, 36, 47B, 55BR; University of Wales, Bangor, Collection in Gwynedd Museum, 68B; Welsh Rugby Union Archives, 157C; West Glamorgan Archive Service, 79T; Williamson Art Gallery and Museum, 78

Artwork

All original artwork by Brett Breckon and Olwen Fowler.

Quotations

Original sources have been translated or simplified into modern English where necessary. The publishers would like to thank the following for permission to use quotations from their work:
Janet Davies (*The Welsh Language: Pocket Guide*), Russell Davies (*Secret Sins*), Peter Gaunt, Matthew Griffiths ('Land, Life and Belief, 1415–1642'), Gareth Elwyn Jones (*Tudor Wales*), the estate of Beti Rhys, John Simkin (*Wales in Industrial Britain*).

The authors and publishers wish to thank the following for their expert and invaluable advice during the preparation of this volume:

Members of the Advisory Committee for this Project:
David Maddox, ESIS
Gwawr Meirion, Ysgol Glan Clwyd, St Asaph
Michael Riley, Bath Spa University College and Associate Consultant for History, Somerset LEA

Members of the Monitoring Panel for ACCAC

Our thanks go also to the history teachers and pupils of the following schools for trialling some of the material:
King Henry VIII School, Abergavenny
Mary Immaculate RC High School, Cardiff
Pencoed Comprehensive School, Bridgend
Ysgol Gyfun Cwm Rhymni, Fleur de Lys
Ysgol Morgan Llwyd, Wrexham
Ysgol Syr Hugh Owen, Caernarfon

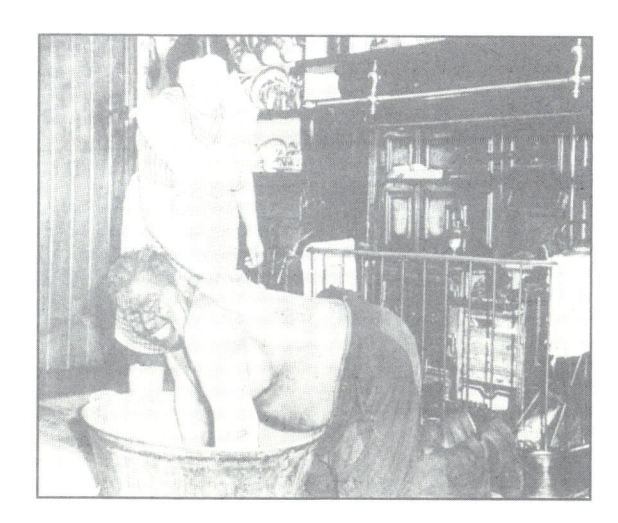

J942.9